PRAISE I

"Dr. Cosby's fundamental work is lighting a path for pastors, activists, and community members who are committed to an interpretation of Scripture that specifically defines our predicament as a tyrannized group and daringly confronts our oppressors.

In *Getting to the Promised Land*, Dr. Cosby gifts us with a new lens through which to understand and utilize the Bible. He has developed the essential biblical hermeneutic for Black clergy members looking to understand the situation of American Descendants of Slavery (ADOS) in the twenty-first century and make the Word of God maximally relevant to their congregations."

—**YVETTE CARNELL**, cofounder of the ADOS movement (ADOS); founder and host of Breaking Brown YouTube channel; former congressional aide to Senator Barbara Boxer (D-CA) and, later, former Congressman Marion Berry (D-AR); author of articles that have appeared in *The Huffington Post*, *Counterpunch*, and YourBlackWorld; and featured guest on national news outlets, including *The Nation*, *The Guardian*, *Politico*, and NPR

"Dr. Cosby takes the foundational elements of ADOS concepts and weaves in theology with a unique and daring perspective. Reading *Getting to the Promised Land* definitely pushes us forward on the road to reparative justice."

—**ANTONIO MOORE**, cofounder of the ADOS movement, attorney in Los Angeles, coproducer of the Emmy-nominated documentary *Crack in the System* presented by Al Jazeera, and host of a weekly radio show called *Tonetalks* that covers issues from mass incarceration to wealth inequality

"Reparations for centuries of racist structural obstacles to African American capital formation is a subject of great controversy today. A crucial aspect of that question is who among Black Americans should be eligible for reparative relief. In an exciting paradigm shift, Kevin Cosby eschews the biblical Exodus motif that is usually invoked with regard to Black America's plight and instead presents a passionate, cogently argued case for using the prophet Nehemiah and the Bible's post-exilic accounts to contend that, rather than all Black people in America, only those who are the descendants of racially enslaved Americans should be eligible for such relief. This is a brilliantly thoughtful, novel approach to the reparations debate that should be required reading for everyone with even a minimal investment in that debate. Kudos to Kevin Cosby for this timely, crucial intervention."

—**OBERY HENDRICKS**, Professor of Religion and African American and Afro-Diasporic Studies, Columbia University; and author of *Christians against Christianity: How Right-Wing Evangelicals Are Destroying Our Nation and Our Faith*

"Kevin Cosby has forcefully traced out the distinct identity, suffering, and future of American Descendants of Slavery (ADOS). The distinctiveness of this identity is to refuse any more 'comfortable' identification as 'Afro-Americans,' as the history and identity of erstwhile US slaves that matters in their long abusive bondage is 'American,' not African. Cosby shrewdly rereads Scripture that pivots around the figure of Nehemiah, the key figure in the restoration of displaced Israel. His reading of Scripture helps to illuminate both the history to which ADOS have been subjected and the prospects for restoration and rehabilitation in American society. Because the issues for ADOS are largely economic (being 'cheap labor' for so long!), Cosby is compelling in his insistence that restoration of ADOS into US society must include reparations. This hard-hitting book is a welcome continuation of our education in the truth of our common history and is an urgent read for all those who care about the future of our society. I am glad to commend the book and its courageous author."

—**WALTER BRUEGGEMANN**, William Marcellus McPheeters Professor Emeritus of Old Testament, Columbia Theological Seminary; an ordained minister in the United Church of Christ; and author of dozens of books, including *Sabbath as Resistance: Saying No to the Culture of Now*, *Interrupting Silence: God's Command to Speak Out*, and *Truth and Hope: Essays for a Perilous Age*

"As foundational truths about our country's historical trajectory of enslavement and dehumanization of African Americans are trying to be replaced with 'alternative facts,' Dr. Cosby calls us to reorient our moral, ethical, and theological compass toward the distinct experience of descendants of slaves. This harrowing experience stands alone in US history and must not be morphed into an amalgamation of oppressions that seek to universalize suffering. Fixing our gaze on the particular plight of African American people and making restitution for the centuries of economic exploitation and human degradation will move us closer to the truth that will set us all free. Nothing less than this will do."

—**LEAH GUNNING FRANCIS**, Vice President for Academic Affairs and Dean of the Faculty, Christian Theological Seminary, Indianapolis, Indiana; and author of *Ferguson and Faith: Sparking Leadership and Awakening Community*

"*Getting to the Promised Land* gives powerful thought to the search for a new strategic vision for Black liberation and to the national debate over reparations. Dr. Cosby, distinguished pastor and president of Simmons College in Kentucky, deftly employs the less-known life of the Hebrew prophet Nehemiah to animate the author's own vision of liberation and reparations and to empower the movement he helped create to further his vision. Dr. Cosby's wisdom, moral passion, and gift for storytelling make this an essential work for the Black world and the wider world as well."

—**STEWART BURNS**, Professor of Ethical & Creative Leadership and of Martin Luther King Studies, Union Institute & University; and author of the Wilbur Award-winning biography of Martin Luther King, *To the Mountaintop*

"Dr. Kevin Cosby has masterfully reimagined theology by intentionally focusing on the experiences of ADOS. His book is a much-needed wake-up call for everyone but especially for followers of Jesus committed to Black liberation and reparations for ADOS. In the same way that Dr. James Cone's brilliant mind gave birth to Black liberation theology, Dr. Cosby's refreshing treatment of Black liberation theology that is ADOS-centric challenges, reproves, and exhorts us to reenvision realities and possibilities. WOW!"

—**WENDELL GRIFFEN**, Pastor, New Millennium Church, Little Rock, Arkansas; Arkansas trial judge; consultant in cultural competency and inclusion; and author of *The Fierce Urgency of Prophetic Hope*

"Dr. Kevin Cosby's book is the clearest articulation and the most compelling argument, from a Christian perspective, of the nature of the ADOS movement and its legitimate claim for equity and reparations. Founded by Yvette Brown and Antonio Moore, the ADOS movement is a grassroots effort that is arguably the most significant struggle for justice in the Black struggle for freedom in America. Dr. Cosby maintains that the ADOS movement is the legitimate heir to the original intent of Martin Luther Kings's work in the civil rights movement. And he insists that every Black church, still committed to its legacy as a leader in the Black freedom struggle, should be a partner in the ADOS effort. To make his case, Cosby ingeniously argues that the church must make a paradigm shift from Moses to Nehemiah for best insights into moving forward in the struggle. His book is a courageous, thought-provoking, truth-telling work that is centered in Christ, supported by Scripture, bathed in love, rooted in hope, and committed to completing the work for real justice for ADOS."

—**F. BRUCE WILLIAMS**, Senior Pastor, Bates Memorial Baptist Church, Louisville, Kentucky

"In this important book, distinguished preacher and teacher Dr. Kevin Cosby introduces a theology of ADOS. Rather than using the narrative of Exodus and liberation, Cosby mines the stories of Nehemiah and the return of the Jews to rebuild Jerusalem after the exile. As he calls ADOS to the work of repair, he calls the white community to the work of reparations. This book will challenge many to rethink what the next steps must look like in rebuilding Black institutions and communities."

—**CYNTHIA M. CAMPBELL**, President emerita, McCormick Theological Seminary; and retired Pastor, Highland Presbyterian Church, Louisville, Kentucky

"In his book *Getting to the Promised Land*, Kevin Cosby provides keen insight and a spiritual, social, and moral challenge to face with integrity the ongoing struggle for social justice and empowerment of the Black community. His argument for reparations gives clarity that Black people are not beggars but builders who make their claim for equal access to the resources that make for a usable future. In this remarkable work, Cosby calls for contemporary leaders to remember that after four hundred years of free labor white America wrote a check to Black America that came back marked insufficient funds. Religious, social, and civic leaders today must continue to call our nation to a place of accountability. God bless Dr. Kevin Cosby for this challenging and inspirational book!"

—**WALTER MALONE JR.**, Pastor and Founder, Canaan Christian Church, Louisville, Kentucky

Getting to the Promised Land

Black America and the Unfinished Work of the Civil Rights Movement

Kevin W. Cosby

WESTMINSTER
JOHN KNOX PRESS
LOUISVILLE • KENTUCKY

First edition
Published by Westminster John Knox Press
Louisville, Kentucky

21 22 23 24 25 26 27 28 29 30—10 9 8 7 6 5 4 3 2 1

Book design by Sharon Adams
Cover design by Nita Ybarra

Library of Congress Cataloging-in-Publication Data

Names: Cosby, Kevin W., author.
Title: Getting to the promised land : Black America and the unfinished work of the civil rights movement / Kevin W. Cosby.
Description: First edition. | Louisville, Kentucky : Westminster John Knox Press, 2021. | Summary: "Pointing to the stories of Nehemiah, Daniel, Solomon, and other biblical leaders for guidance on how to rebuild Black America, Kevin W. Cosby challenges all Americans to move from a place of relative nonengagement and detachment to a place of active support of the American Descendants of Slavery's (ADOS) efforts for justice and healing"-- Provided by publisher.
Identifiers: LCCN 2021011147 (print) | LCCN 2021011148 (ebook) | ISBN 9780664265458 (paperback) | ISBN 9781646981977 (ebook)
Subjects: LCSH: African American leadership. | African Americans--Civil rights. | Leadership in the Bible. | African Americans--Reparations | United States--Race relations.
Classification: LCC E185 .C763 2021 (print) | LCC E185 (ebook) | DDC 323.1196/073--dc23
LC record available at https://lccn.loc.gov/2021011147
LC ebook record available at https://lccn.loc.gov/2021011148

Most Westminster John Knox Press books are available at special quantity discounts when purchased in bulk by corporations, organizations, and special-interest groups. For more information, please e-mail SpecialSales@wjkbooks.com.

This book is dedicated to St. Stephen Baptist Church, an institution that has never wavered from the historic mission of the Black church to promote ADOS group empowerment and ADOS group political advocacy. May we continue to infuse those values into our collective experience.

Contents

Foreword

I n the Reverend Dr. Kevin Cosby, the ADOS movement has a true love warrior. And when I talk about love warriors, I am speaking about a specific group of folk who really love the people. You see, when you genuinely love folk, you hate the fact that they are being treated unfairly; you loathe the fact that they are being treated unjustly. And you know that if you don't do something about it, then the rocks are going to shout out! That is the tradition that we in the Black freedom struggle come from. And so it is in these consecrated pages written by our dear brother Kevin Cosby.

Dr. Cosby understands that reparations is about two things. First, it is about truth. And he knows that the condition of truth is that *you must allow the suffering to speak.* Second, reparations is about justice; it is about understanding where the damage is, who did it, and then where that offending party needs to direct the repair. The Black freedom struggle in America, from the very beginning, has always been in pursuit of these two things: truth and justice. And reparations is simply one of the ways in which our quest for truth, and our quest for justice, is brought to bear on white supremacy—an ideology that says Black history is a curse, Black freedom is a pipe dream, and Black hope is a joke.

Now of course we know that is not the case. We come from a great people. We come from a grand tradition. There is no other group of people in the modern world who've been terrorized under slavery and Jim Crow Jr. and Jim Crow Sr. and who have still—despite these horrible experiences—taught the world so much about *freedom*. There is no other group of people who have been traumatized for four hundred years and still manage to teach the world so much about *healing*. You can hear it in our music; you can see it in the way we connect with one another. And while we as a people have been hated so chronically, institutionally, and systematically for four hundred years, we have nonetheless taught the world so much about how to love. Just turn on John Coltrane's "Love Supreme" or Marvin Gaye's "What's Going On?" Listen to Stevie Wonder's "Love's in Need of Love Today," or read James Baldwin's love-soaked essays or Toni Morrison's *Beloved*; see Mama on the stage in *Raisin in the Sun* and see how there's never been a character on the American stage full of so much love in the history of the whole nation, in the history of the whole empire! And what Kevin Cosby's book proves is that there ain't no stopping us now.

Brother Cosby proceeds from this fundamental truth: that you don't love Black people because you want them to love you back; no, you love them because *they're worthy of being loved*. And just like tenderness is what love feels like in private, justice is what love looks like in public.

Somewhere I read that love takes away your fear, that love takes away your intimidation. In the Black community we used to have churches and mosques where we had genuine, fearless leaders. The problem is that in the 1960s so many of our love warriors were assassinated or incarcerated. And we ended up with polished professionals who acted as if they were leaders when what they really wanted to be was well-adjusted to injustice.

I'm reminded about how there used to be a brother named Sylvester on the organ in my church every fifth Sunday, but he's known to the world for the genius that he is as Sly Stone. And Sly Stone wrote a song that went "Stand! There's a cross for you to bear, things to go through if you going anywhere." In other words, we don't need cowards or conformers. If you're scared, get out of the way. Now that's old school, and what's beautiful is that today we got new school here. The ADOS movement is the new school, and in this book Brother Cosby brings a new interpretation of the book of Nehemiah to undergird and inform the righteousness of this new movement of love, of truth, of justice.

People have said that the ADOS movement is flawed because they're being so specific when they talk about their group being so distinctive. People say that the ADOS movement is about putting other folk down. But read Kevin Cosby's words in this book and I believe that you'll come away with a much deeper and honest understanding about what this movement really signifies. At its core, Kevin Cosby's book is talking about love. Brother Cosby knows that you don't love Black people by putting other folk down. That's white supremacy! Those who espouse white supremacy stand tall by trying to keep us on our knees. We love each other *in and of itself.* And then, when the love spills over, it's even more real. But let me tell you this: we are in a moment where the polished professionals too often love everybody *but* Black people. That's what I can't stand. Oh no, now I'm a Christian. Now, I love everybody, and I'm gonna be faithful unto death, but I'm gonna tell you this: I'm loving the chocolate side first. How can I not? How can I love the other side if I don't love myself? Love your neighbor *as* yourself. Learn how to love yourself and then love your neighbor, and it will necessarily spill over.

ADOS has got nothing against other Black people. They know that Caribbeans and African folk are beautiful too, but that as ADOS we need to love ourselves, and in so doing we can then make sure the love is equally spread. That's what I believe Dr. Cosby's book is here to tell the world. This book demonstrates to us, above all, the importance of loving ourselves first, so that we may properly love others.

Cornel West

Preface

Martin Luther King Jr. was assassinated less than twenty-four hours after he gave what many consider to be the greatest speech of his life. And in what is now both a poignant and strikingly premonitory aspect of that speech, King reflects on his own mortality, alluding to a scene from the Bible: "Like any man, I would like to live a long life," he says. "Longevity has its place. But I'm not concerned about that now. I just want to do God's will. And He's allowed me to go up to the mountain. And I've looked over. And I've seen the promised land. I may not get there with you. But I want you to know tonight, that we, as a people, will get to the promised land."[1]

That line—"we, as a people, will get to the promised land"—has occupied a permanent place in my mind. Indeed, it is no great exaggeration to say that my whole life, in one way or another, has been consumed by trying to understand the deeper implications of what King is saying in these words and how they express his sublime vision of the Black freedom struggle in America. What I've come to believe is that "we, as a people, will get to the promised land" synthesizes the most important aspects of his political thought, and that those characteristics furthermore provide the essential model of leadership for those who, like myself, are intensely engaged in the continuation of that struggle, and who aim to help see Dr. King's unfinished work through to completion.

For the last five years, I have been at the fore of a national racial justice movement made up of the American Descendants of Slavery, or ADOS. The movement's principal objective is to show how the *full cost* of what it means to be Black in America is knowable and calculable only through a person's lineage, as opposed to his or her skin color. This makes a necessary distinction between those in the Black American community who trace their lineage to chattel slavery and those whose families voluntarily immigrated to the United States.[2] By specifically focusing on the former group's unique identity and history in America, the ADOS movement can thus most effectively carry on King's legacy: namely, working to obtain the rights of full citizenship for ADOS through a political agenda whose core demand is reparations.

In October 2019, the college of which I am the president—Simmons College of Kentucky, the commonwealth's oldest HBCU (Historically Black Colleges and Universities)—hosted the first national ADOS conference. Over two thousand people from across the country attended the event. Among the speakers were the movement's two founders, Yvette Carnell and Antonio Moore; Rep. John Yarmuth, chairman of the House Budget Committee; legendary activist and philosopher Cornel West; and then Democratic presidential candidate Marianne Williamson. The *New York Times* assigned a reporter to cover the proceedings, and an article detailing the movement's growth graced the paper's front page the following month. A few months later, ABC News aired a segment about ADOS in which they introduced their viewership to the budding justice movement.

My involvement with the ADOS movement has been marked by a religio-political coherence previously unknown to me. That the movement has found an institutional hub here in Louisville, Kentucky, at my church and college is indicative of the critical role that I believe our institutions (particularly the Black church) need to play in our ongoing freedom struggle. The interplay between Black institutions and our demand for meaningful inclusion into the United States is central to a theological framework that I have developed in recent years and which uses the gospel to support

ADOS's particular justice claim. From the very beginning, there was great synergy between the ADOS movement and an initiative I started in 2015 called The Angela Project. In association with the National Baptist Convention of America, the Cooperative Baptist Fellowship, and the Progressive Baptist Convention, The Angela Project was meant to commemorate the four hundredth anniversary of Black enslavement in America, and, in so doing, help educate and mobilize a millions-strong multiracial coalition in the faith-based community to advocate for ADOS in their political fight for economic justice.

This is not to say, however, that my past affinities and forays into various Afro-philosophies have not yielded me great insight into who I am as a Black person of faith in particular, and also what it means to be a Black person in America more generally. Indeed, it is precisely *because* of those past intellectual pilgrimages that I feel I possess an even fuller appreciation for where I am now in my journey.

From the time I was a young boy in Louisville, Kentucky, my parents worked to instill in me a heightened awareness of—and commitment to—our group's struggle for racial justice in America. To study Black history was a requirement in our home. My father served as president of the NAACP's Louisville branch. My mother, who was a professional pianist, taught the instrument to Darlene and Vernon King, the niece and nephew of Martin Luther King Jr. And, on several occasions, I recall both he and his father, Martin Luther King Sr., visiting my childhood home.

However, it was not enough to just study Black history. I knew that—since our history is so much a part of our present—one must use his or her life as an opportunity to contribute to it as well. So, at the age of nineteen, while attending Eastern Kentucky University as a history major, I started the student chapter of the EKU branch of the NAACP. In Madison County, where EKU is located, I also established its NAACP county branch, which is still in existence today.

During my senior year, I became the pastor of the 175-member St. Stephen Baptist Church, where I worshiped as a child and currently serve as senior pastor. The church of St. Stephen is in West Louisville's California neighborhood. California is the poorest zip code in the state of Kentucky, and it ranks as one of the poorest and most segregated urban areas in all of America. Today, with over twelve thousand members, St. Stephen has the distinction of being the largest African American church in Kentucky.

Upon graduating from EKU, I enrolled in Louisville's Southern Baptist Theological Seminary. There, I intended to incorporate as much "Black-Church History" and "Black-Historical Theology" into my studies as I could. These Black-centric courses were not offered during the regular semester, but rather as electives during the J-terms of January, June, and July, a testament to the marginalization of the Black experience in mainstream white institutions. Indeed, it was that feature of the curriculum (along with the fact of "Black" being hyphenated in the titles of these disciplines) that would prove decisive in shaping both my outlook on society and my religious praxis and practice. I began to realize the extent of the ideology behind creating and sustaining the norm of the white experience in America and the less obvious ways in which anything that wasn't white was meant to be portrayed as abnormal.

In the early 1990s I enrolled in United Theological Seminary to pursue a doctoral degree in Afrocentric studies. The Afrocentrists believe that Black Americans must recognize the supposedly natural affinity they have with traditional African culture. And, in reclaiming that dimension of cultural Africanism, Black Americans can thus unite in solidarity with other persons throughout the Black diaspora in order to create alternative and putatively more authentic modes of being within a paradigm of Western hegemony. My dissertation aimed to bring together William Cross's racial-ethnic identity development philosophy and *Nigrescence*—a French term meaning "conversion to black"—to discover ways by which we might use the Black church as a vehicle to facilitate the conversion in which Blacks become less Eurocentric in their orientation, and more Afrocentric.

As is apparent, Afrocentrism has had a profound impact on me as a person and in my development as a thinker. It infused in me a necessary conviction that I, as a person of African descent, am exceptional. Having grown up in a society that had sought to shape my perception of Africa as being a continent of savagery and inferiority, I found this new perspective helped me to see how I had been a victim of "conceptual incarceration": that is, how I, as a Black person, had been taught to view life chiefly through a white lens. Afrocentrism encouraged me to celebrate my dark skin and my kinky hair. The more I immersed myself in the philosophy, the more I began to see everything through a *Black* lens. The Eurocentric images of God and Jesus, the biblical imagery depicted by artists of the Renaissance—all of this became intolerable for me. In fact, so great was Afrocentrism's influence, I even began to refer to myself as *Bandele*, which means "child who is born away from home."

I will always be indebted to Afrocentrism. However, as my thinking evolved, I eventually became aware of its inherent limitations for the descendants of American chattel slavery. Apart from the suspect historiography at its core (namely, that Africa can be so easily abstracted into a neatly unified continent, an imaginary place in which there are not in fact many different countries, all with myriad cultures that are distinct to each), Afrocentric politics are diametrically opposed to the political agenda of the civil rights movement led by Martin Luther King Jr. For King, the civil rights movement—particularly the emergence of Black Power—had helped eradicate the pernicious idea in a Black person's head that they were a "nobody," that their Blackness was a "sign of [their] biological depravity," or that it meant their "being [had] been stamped with an indelible imprint of inferiority."[3]

To use King's own phrase, the civil rights movement had given the Black person a sense of "somebody-ness."

Of course, the Afrocentrist would not likely object to this statement. However, where Dr. King would part with the Afrocentrist is on the issue of identity and agenda. Describing how these two things are ultimately anchored in America, King once wrote, "Every man must ultimately confront the question 'who am I?' and seek to answer it honestly." He continued,

The Negro's greatest dilemma is that in order to be healthy he must accept his ambivalence. The Negro is a child of two cultures—Africa and America. The problem is that in the search for wholeness all too many Negroes seek to embrace only one side of their natures. . . . The American Negro is neither totally African nor totally Western. He is Afro-American, a true hybrid, a combination of two cultures. . . . In spite of the psychological appeals of identification with Africa, the Negro must face the fact that America is now his home, a home that he helped build through "blood, sweat and tears."[4]

That conviction was the reason that King, prior to his assassination, had been in Memphis for two months trying to secure economic and workplace justice for the city's Black sanitation workers. That conviction—that America owes its Black population descended from slaves—was why the year leading up to his time in Memphis had been one of such tremendous personal strife for King. It was why a full 72 percent of white Americans had an unfavorable view of him, and why he had received multiple death threats and suffered numerous attempts on his life.[5] In fact, the airplane on which he had flown to Memphis had been delayed from taking off because it had to be searched for a possible bomb.

As a leading advocate for economic justice for ADOS, Martin Luther King Jr. was a lightning rod for white America's murderous hostility to the idea of meaningfully atoning for its legacy of racism. White society would much rather focus on, and elevate, an exceptional Black who has beaten the odds and risen above racism and poverty to become successful. But Dr. King was not concerned about Blacks who managed to beat the odds. Rather, he was committed to doing all that he could to reduce the odds of poverty for the Black masses in America. It was not *me* the people, but *we* the people. And while King no doubt believed in justice for all oppressed people, he nonetheless recognized how Black descendants of slavery and Jim Crow had a special justice claim with the US government.

Today, American society attempts to overlook this fact, instead preferring to group all oppressed people under the moniker "people of color." However, to blend ADOS into such a coalition only serves to diminish that group's unique history and the attendant justice claim. ADOS is, after all, the only group whose ancestors were forcibly brought to America against their will. ADOS is, after all, the only group in America whose people were made slaves. And ADOS is, after all, the only group in America against which laws were passed to repeatedly and specifically exclude them from the social, political, and economic rights that are supposed to accompany American citizenship. This is what Dr. King fought against, and it is the fight which we today must continue. And for it, we—like King—must be willing to lose everything without a moment's hesitation.

As a member of the baby boomer generation, I was born prior to the landmark civil rights legislation of the 1960s. Today, many boomers are passing from the scene. And it is perhaps only natural to find myself on occasion contemplating my own impermanence here on earth and the legacy that I will leave behind. Presently, the group to which I belong is a bottom caste in American society. This, in fact, has always been the place we were made to occupy. And for every dollar that whites possess, ADOS hold only ten cents. Not surprisingly—since society is always eager to justify inequality by assigning defects to the victims of inequality rather than to the system that produces it—there are many who like to believe that disparity reflects the fact that ADOS are poor simply because we make "bad choices." But in fact that utter absence of wealth within ADOS is more appropriately understood as a direct result of centuries of draconian, often state-sanctioned practices that specifically exploited and excluded us. The reality, then, is that it has never been about the choices that ADOS make but about the choices that ADOS *have*.

It goes without saying that many of my people are not afforded a plethora of choices. But as a leader in the ADOS community, I am saying it. Thus, it is incumbent upon me to make certain that my choices are made with an eye toward increasing the availability of choices for the group. My decision to write this book, which I hope will honor the legacy of Martin Luther King Jr. and help facilitate the completion of his righteous justice work for ADOS, is one such choice. It is a choice made specifically *for* my group, because I too believe that, while I might not get there with you, *we* will get to the promised land.

Kevin Cosby
September 2020

Introduction

In America, a certain tension has long characterized the relationship between Black political activism and Christian doctrine as it is traditionally preached throughout the country. That conflict, perhaps, is to be expected. After all, given the ongoing oppression of the Black population in the United States, it is reasonable to question Christianity's relevance when it is so ambivalent toward those numerous violences and existing iniquities.

On one hand, it is a Christianity that claims to reprove such injustice. And yet, if one visits any number of Black churches across America, that person will surely observe how that same Christianity seems to merely counsel us (the principal victims, no less) to exercise patience and forbearance while living under precisely those conditions of provocation. This version of Christianity curiously encourages its Black congregations to accept that the fulfilment of their freedom is to be found in eternal salvation, this despite our nation's apparent bedrock of truth that God has endowed each and every one of us with the right to liberty *here* on earth. What are we supposed to make, then, of a Christianity that remains essentially reticent about the fact that from the very beginning, with respect to its Black population, the United States has acted in direct contradiction to that supposed belief? Rather, it has sought to radically attenuate the "freedom" of our community to the point of meaninglessness.

1

Given these circumstances, how are we ever to see the message of Christ and the collective effort to free ourselves from oppression as being divinely consistent with one another?

In his seminal work, *Black Theology and Black Power*, Rev. Dr. James Cone confronted these questions of compatibility head-on. He forcefully argued the essential emancipatory nature of Jesus' ministry and demonstrated how the Black freedom struggle, with its aim of liberating Black people and setting them on a course of self-determination, embodied a distinctly Christian mission. In so doing, Dr. Cone established the theological underpinnings for a religion that could meaningfully engage with our people's resistance to exploitation and injustice. This Christianity recognized the singularity of the Black experience in the United States and respected the indissolubility of Black identity: "It is impossible for me to surrender this basic reality [of Blackness] for a 'higher, more universal' reality," Cone wrote. "Therefore, if a higher, Ultimate reality is to have meaning, it must relate to the very essence of blackness."[1] This was Cone's governing proposition, and for him it would locate God at the very core of Black liberation as realized through Black Power, a conception of freedom described by Stokely Carmichael wherein Blacks are controlling the economics, education, and politics in the Black community.

There can be no doubt, however, that in the United States of America today (now nearly fifty years since Carmichael articulated that sublime vision of the Black community in full possession of their own affairs in national life), we fall woefully short in actually inhabiting such a space. Nowhere is this lamentable scenario more obvious than in the present-day wealth gap that divides white America from Black America. For the former group, the median wealth stands at $120,000. For African Americans, it is an astoundingly low $1,700 when you subtract depreciating assets such as the family car.[2] This disparity is naturally reflected in our homeownership rates, which, at 41.3 percent in 2016, marked the lowest number recorded in fifty years. That very same year it was also reported that African Americans were the only racial group earning *less* than they had been at the turn of the century.[3] Whites, Asians, and Latinx all saw gains in their incomes at the median, while Black median income languished at its pre-2000 level. And while President Trump touted record-low unemployment numbers for Blacks, this apparently laudable achievement conceals the millions of Black men whom our criminal justice system has, over the last several decades, committed to prisons at rates unequaled in the modern world. In lauding "record-low" Black unemployment, we celebrate nothing so much as the terrifying adaptability of our institutions to simply absent the Black man from American society.

All of which is to say that in virtually every area of racial progress, we have reverted to a much darker period in our nation's history. And yet we seem today surer than ever of our supposedly improved race relations. We have a sense of progress that is totally at odds with what the available data tells us about ourselves and our present condition. The question we must consider is how have we arrived at such a point of deep contradiction? How is it that the gesture of the closed, raised fist that signifies Black Power (while no doubt defiant and evocative of the historic struggle out of slavery and an overcoming of its legacy of seemingly insuperable odds) is a fist that has *never truly held the economic power for which it is owed*? More importantly, how do we interpret this situation religiously? Dr. Cone wrote, "While the gospel itself does not change, every generation is confronted with new problems, and the gospel must be brought to bear on them."[4] If this is true, then ought we not be critical of the orthodox consensus shaped by Christian intellectuals of a totally different time—intellectuals whose interpretations of the Scripture may not address our current predicament? Is a reevaluation of Black theology necessary in order to point the way toward a new horizon of possibility for Black people in America? And if so, then what religious ideas are now required to further Black people in our aim of freedom in order to facilitate, as Dr. Cone wrote, "[our] becoming what [our] Creator intended"?[5]

It is my contention that Black America in 2020 is standing upon the threshold of tremendous possibility. And that if we are to imagine a theology that seeks to meaningfully involve the Christian doctrine in the current stage of our struggle, then the principal task before us is to recover the meaning of "the very essence of blackness" of which Dr. Cone spoke, and to properly anchor that in the American context in order to understand our condition as a population uniquely excluded. After all, if we accept Cone's premise that what separates true Christianity from false doctrine is the former's ability to connect to the core of our experience as Black people in America, it then would seem to greatly behoove us to incorporate *new* knowledge and *new* insights gleaned from the last half century into our analysis of what exactly distinguishes our experience today in national life.

Writing in the 1960s, Dr. Cone said that our condition as Black Americans was defined by "living under unbearable oppression."[6] While that description no doubt rings true yet today, the need to speak of that oppression in the most precise terms possible is now more urgent than ever. What I hope to communicate in the following pages is that if we fail to identify the *specific* manner in which we as a group have been made to inhabit our circumstance in America (namely, that abhorrent racial caste system in which we are accorded status in the *exact inverse relation* to our ancestors' great contributions to this country), our group's efforts at freedom from that condition will be all naught.

Avoiding this fate will require us to reevaluate what it means to be Black in America. Of course, we must adhere to Dr. Cone's injunction that we cannot lay aside that most salient fact of our experience—that "basic reality" of our Blackness—in favor of some universal alternative. However, in a critical way, we must also recognize the ways in which Blackness itself has become a de-particularized and quasi-universal concept of exactly the sort that Cone himself warned would diminish our relation to the sort of radical Christianity that would aid us in fulfilling our destiny of earthly freedom.

In other words, the way forward will require us to get very honest about the fact that while the tapestry of Blackness in the United States has grown evermore rich in the twenty-first century, it is the American Descendants of Slavery (ADOS) who, as a group, remain its poorest expression. And if we are to see in Scripture that which is analogous to our struggle in the present, we must first and foremost recall that our struggle as ADOS is, in its essence, a singular one. Therefore, our identity must be understood in the particular as well. Because while it is true that the essence of our Blackness is in part the tragedy of being made to occupy a station in life so obscenely incommensurate with what should be our rightful inheritance as ADOS, it is in equal if not greater part a *justice-driven* essence. As a group we have perpetually striven toward this end against such tremendous odds and against the most un-Christian instincts of this country. Our identity, which is anchored in the dramatic totality of economic exclusion from American society, has necessarily demanded it.

Today we encounter new obstacles that complicate our cause. We must contend with not only a rapidly changing set of demographics within the nation but also a rigid attitude toward that shift that prefers to see all Black people—whether native born or immigrant—as being impacted by systemic racism in essentially the same way. It appears the intent is to lump together all Black people who reside in America—whether they be ADOS or immigrants from Africa and Latin America—just because we bear a superficial likeness to one another. Such an inclusive project, however, threatens to postpone justice indefinitely for ADOS and only hasten our destruction as a people. There is also today, more so than ever, a dogmatic insistence that ADOS conform to the sort of partisan politics that have so obviously produced nothing in the way of positive outcomes for our group.

However, a countervailing and corrective force has emerged in response to this host of factors deepening the wedge between ADOS identity and its attendant, *specific* demand of economic justice. The ADOS movement declares lineage to be the organizing principle in a grassroots campaign for reparative justice. That is, American Descendants of Slavery—as the only group to have experienced the whole spectrum of economic exclusion from chattel slavery and Jim Crow to redlining and mass incarceration—have a unique justice claim in the United States. By clarifying this, ADOS has effectively cleared a new path forward on which to recommence the Black freedom struggle in America. ADOS offers a form of unique fellowship among the forgotten through an identity that gathers the group under one coherent history and experience—namely, a shutting out of possibility maintained across generations. It reaffirms that history and experience at a critical moment.

And so just as the moment in 2021 demands a decisive break from a body of established opinion and political thought that has patently reversed our progress over the last half century, so too do we now find ourselves at a theological crossroads with similar implications. As I intend to demonstrate, a Black theology that stubbornly clings to an interpretation of Christian doctrine that is against a conception of liberation as embodied by ADOS is one that necessarily consigns itself to irrelevance to the American Descendants of Slavery who today are struggling to survive in the United States. In the ADOS movement's call for a collective reorientation away from the decoys of multiculturalism and toward a program of political action anchored in our particular cultural memory, there is an undeniable sense of something vital. Something that, for so long, has been kept apart from our experience, and which is now rupturing into our present so as to properly shape our political response to the moment. It is a thing from which we have been made to feel estranged but which nonetheless has endured faithfully. It has preserved the whole past that makes up our community as one people, one tribe. Now newly arrived and articulated most forcibly by the ADOS movement's cofounders, Yvette Carnell and Antonio Moore, it provides us with much needed placement—a feeling of home, belonging, and determined intention. In many ways what the ADOS movement is aiming to do is the very thing for which authentic ministry should always strive: to introduce the congregation to its *undiscovered self*. And by doing that, give the people the power to pursue what they already know to be true. As ADOS works both locally and nationally to bring our group toward that profound encounter with our undiscovered self, we will need our leaders to cooperate with us and work to strengthen our institutions so that we are able to have our will expressed at the highest levels of power in this country. Naturally, the Black church has a crucial role to play among the ranks of leadership in helping bring about this transformative state of affairs, one that sees the interests of our group as the ultimate object to be considered, as that which lies beyond all others and constitutes the final aim.

I believe the church's efforts in this regard will be helped considerably by bringing a fresh perspective to one of the Old Testament's most justice- and group-centered leaders: Nehemiah. While correctly understanding him as a figure who is wholly devoted to the advancement of his tribe in Jerusalem, traditional interpretation of Nehemiah has presupposed this identification with his people to have been a constant throughout his privileged experience in Babylon. However, for a Black liberation theology that is invested in making Scripture maximally relevant to ADOS in the twenty-first century, this account lacks a necessary nuance. Nehemiah was initially unaware of the situation of his people. His story is one of discovery and change and radical action. It is in fact in the arc of consciousness by which Nehemiah arrives at that unwavering loyalty that we as American Descendants of Slavery are able to witness in him a process of self-discovery and focused action not at all dissimilar from what is now required to further our cause.

That trajectory from a place of relative nonengagement and detachment to a place of committed, justice-minded leadership of the oppressed is a mode of *becoming* and *belonging* that Dr. Michael Eric Dyson describes as becoming "intentionally black."[7] Intentional Blackness is a mindset in which ADOS commit themselves to a course of action grounded in the awareness that their specific identity is part of a greater shared history and experience in this country. Dyson posits this as one of three optional subjectivities available to Black individuals in America today, the other two being "accidental blackness," in which persons attribute their blackness to mere chance, preferring instead to emphasize other qualities beyond their Black skin as that which constitute their identity, and "incidental blackness," which incorporates a definite degree of pride in Black culture but which, at the same time, sees that pride as but *one* characteristic within a matrix of greater or lesser interests and concerns that make up their personhood.

The flaw in Dyson's formulation, however, is the notion that these "strategies of blackness" (at least for ADOS) are in flux. Dyson even goes so far as to say that they are *necessarily* in flux. As he writes, "These strategies permit black folk to operate in the world with a bit of sanity and grace."[8] It seems to me, however, that the very opposite is true for the ADOS community—that it is insanity to not understand ADOS life in the twenty-first century as that which dictates but *one* strategy of Blackness, definite and fixed and informed entirely by a recognition of how that dimension of our identity—*our Blackness*—was never at any time in our group's history understood by systems of oppression as accidental or incidental.

Indeed, in all three arenas—the political, the economic, and the social—we now see more than ever how our Blackness has always been intentionally made to manifest in a manner of thoroughgoing exclusion. Nothing else—not a single thing in our lives—has so served to determine and fix the extent of what is achievable for our group in America. And so it is neither sanity nor grace but pure recklessness to proceed as though we somehow have the luxury or privilege of transitioning here and there into a less consequential relation to our lineage. Grace would be not only accepting this reality but recognizing that, in the pursuit of justice for being made to inhabit this condition, we as ADOS are decidedly bound by it!

And so let us, beginning now, enter into that pursuit anew, suffused with the awareness that a withdrawal from intentional ADOSness is neither possible nor desirable. In our continued fight for authentic economic inclusion in America, let our spirits be buoyed and our resolve fortified by that basic inescapability of our ADOSness! Because in it is contained the glorious promise of Christ establishing justice here on earth.

Chapter One

Replace the Exodus Hermeneutic with a Postexilic One

Regain a Singular Focus

Foundational to ADOS theology is demonstrating how the post-Babylonian exilic period is the most appropriate biblical referent to help us understand the situation with which we as ADOS are confronted today. Unlike the Exodus model, which has long enjoyed favor among Black preachers, the post-Babylonian exilic period, as we will see, proves exceedingly more relevant to our group's predicament and far more valuable in terms of providing solutions.

The post-Babylonian exilic period refers specifically to the years 537–430 BCE. At the time, Jerusalem was in ruins following its conquest at the hands of the Babylonian army. Prior to that, during the years 596–586 BCE, waves of forced deportations of the population had left those Jews who remained on the land poor and leaderless (Jer. 52:16). In a separate chapter, we will discuss how those deportation efforts—having specifically removed the most educated and economically privileged of the Jewish population in Jerusalem—mirror America's siphoning off of ADOS leadership. However, for our purposes in this chapter, we will look at how, in the absence of Jewish human capital, the remaining Jews were left uniquely vulnerable to the surrounding tribes that Assyria (which had conquered Israel two hundred years earlier) had brought in from other regions and resettled in the nearby provinces. It was these displaced peoples whom the

9

Jerusalemites were made to compete with in order to survive. And it was also these surrounding tribes that would exhibit the greatest opposition to the initiatives to rebuild the city.

This ambitious project of restoration—which was as much about the spiritual as it was the material—was central to the post-Babylonian exilic period. It was undertaken by the once exiled Jews who, having experienced a profound renewal of Jewish faith after the fall of Babylon to the Persians, returned to Jerusalem intending to rebuild the temple that had earlier been destroyed by the Babylonian army when they had first laid siege to the city. Their efforts at rebuilding were continuously hindered, however, owing to both internal and external issues. Externally, the hostilities of the nearby provinces frequently beset the Jews. And within the community itself, the intermarriages that were taking place between the male Jews and the women who belonged to foreign tribes were seen as greatly undermining the Jewish people's collective identity and empowerment. Such arrangements were strongly discouraged under Mosaic law, which, upon their return, the Jews were eager to reinstate in order to help cultivate the people's sense of being a *specific* tribe. On those occasions where marriages to members of a foreign tribe did occur, a severe penalty was imposed: "No Ammonite or Moabite or any of their descendants for ten generations may be admitted to the assembly of the LORD," Deuteronomy 23:3 (NLT) tells us. This was meant to encourage the Jewish people to live their lives in a way that strengthened their bond with God and also to consolidate resources *inside* the community. Indeed, it was principally by way of the foreign tribes' ability to deprive Jewish descendants of land ownership that the economic integrity of the Judean collective was threatened; having violated the precept in Mosaic law that would have guarded against this threat of assimilation, Jerusalem (and the Jewish community in turn) languished.

In other words, it was during the post-Babylonian exilic period when the Jewish people's newfound perception of who they were as a distinct ethnic group became critical to their continued existence. In this way, the period is highly resonant with precisely the kind of realization that American Descendants of Slavery are making today, a realization upon which our group's survival is similarly incumbent.

Nonetheless, much of Black theology today appears content to remain grounded in an Exodus-focused hermeneutic. And as such, those who use it to interpret our struggle do a tremendous disservice to our people. They ill equip us with a model that is incapable of teasing out salient issues of group identification, which is right now so very necessary in terms of informing our collective political action. We cannot continue looking to a biblical model that pertains to a much earlier circumstance for ADOS in this country, a time when white supremacy was in a more rudimentary form. To be sure, while it was equally brutal in outcome, it was far less abstruse in its design and machinations in achieving its primary goal—namely, the total domination of our group. White supremacy today reveals itself to be a remarkably fluid and inclusive system of dominance over ADOS. And in its modern incarnation, "white" is a criterion satisfied less by actual skin color and more by economic advantage relative to the bottommost group in American society. ADOS have always been made to occupy that position. And while today we are encouraged to understand ourselves in a position of disadvantage that uniformly corresponds to other oppressed and marginalized groups, the fact is that there is nothing at all universal or common about the unique condition that has been manufactured for ADOS. The level of immiseration that we experience in America is one that can only be known by *sustained generational inheritance*. Ours is a specific history of exclusion that anti-ADOS public policy ensured would be passed down through our lineage. And while it is our families that continue to inherit that immobilizing economic reality of what it has historically meant to be ADOS, other groups who are not a product of that specific past are able to inherit access to a fuller citizenship. They can realize a level of stability because of the permanence of that basic economic interval between ADOS and everyone else. As such, when staking out our terrain in the political arena, the very first thing we should do is to claim our history as ours *alone*. It needs to be the line we draw in the sand. And insofar as we enter coalitions, we should demand that our plight—which has been made to provide so much in the way of opportunities for others at our expense—be respected as a priority.

Here, the attitudes and strict commitments of the returning Jews in the post-Babylonian exilic period prove instructive. Led by Zerubbabel, who was a grandson of Jehoiachin, a former king of Judah, the first delegation of Jews in Babylon made the pilgrimage back to Jerusalem in 537 BCE. Following the Persian conquest of Babylon, King Cyrus had issued a decree that the Jewish people who had been in Babylonian captivity were to go to Jerusalem and "rebuild the house of the LORD, the God of Israel" (Ezra 1:3). And while the returnees' aim was to rehabilitate the temple, it was at the same time very much a work of Jewish collective empowerment. True, Zerubbabel intended to return to Jerusalem so that the people there would have an appropriate place to worship. However, we cannot say that his focus was only on improving the spiritual lives of the people. Zerubbabel believed that by rebuilding the temple, the community itself would be rebuilt. He believed renewal would ripple outward from the temple, and the people, spiritually rebuilt and fortified, would begin rebuilding their community and institutions. What was unexpected was the reactionary resistance shown by Jerusalem's neighboring enemies.

Shortly after the work on the temple began, Zerubbabel and the workers were approached by neighboring enemies who implored them to allow their participation in the reconstruction. Doubtless the goal of these tribes was to impede the progress that the Jewish community was making for itself. However, to effect this sabotage, they opted for a subtle approach, using the language of solidarity to appeal to an idea of a shared, common project: "Let us help you build," they petitioned, "because, like you, we seek your God and have been sacrificing to him since the time of Esarhaddon king of Assyria, who brought us here" (Ezra 4:2 NIV). At once, Zerubbabel and the workers perceived their deception. For these tribes had never pursued the sort of singular monotheism that God demanded; they merely incorporated "the god of the land" (as they referred to Yahweh) into their pantheon of deities and continued to worship their own gods wherever they settled (2 Kgs. 17:32–33, 41). "You have no part with us in building a temple to our God," Zerubbabel responded to them. "We alone will build it for the LORD, the God of Israel, as King Cyrus, the king of Persia, commanded us" (Ezra 4:3 NIV).

This clear delineation of who is to be included and who is to be excluded from involvement in an oppressed community's restoration efforts is central to ADOS politics. And just as those outsiders sought to infiltrate the Jewish people's movement to rebuild the temple—wishing to hijack it and undermine its long-term interests—so too do other marginalized groups routinely set their sights on the ADOS movement. While their intent might not be to do us explicit harm, the usual outcome of these coalitions (in which we remain a bottom caste while our allies achieve greater inclusion into America) cannot but speak to a hollowness in their core claim that we are united in progress. This is precisely why Yvette Carnell, cofounder of ADOS and founder of the new Black media outlet Breaking Brown, consistently emphasizes how part of establishing a durable movement lies in determining and enforcing who is in and who is out. Exclusion, in other words—as Zerubbabel and the workers recognized—is every bit as important as inclusion.

Our specific history of oppression—the thing for which *we* are owed—has been treated as a steppingstone. It has become, obscenely, the thing that allows other groups to do politics in a way that permits them to contest their place in the supremacy over us. Is it not our fundamental right to object to strategies in which we are just another set of hands in the tug of war against the patriarchy? Against imperialism? Against global capitalism or some other such hegemon? How can we be expected to just empty our hands of the things that we specifically still hold too much of—slavery, Jim Crow, domestic terrorism, lynch mobs, redlining, and mass incarceration—in order to take up others' oppressions and causes? After four hundred years, we can simply no longer enter into such alliance-based enterprises when, in the final analysis, there is no guarantee that we will gain anything.

As ADOS move toward the next decade of the twenty-first

century, and as the situation for our group becomes increasingly dire, we cannot content ourselves with assisting and celebrating the legislative gains of other groups whose strength relative to ours is what inhibits us from participating in coalitions in a recognizably normal manner in the first place. We must demand that we will be the principal beneficiaries in a politics of collaboration. After all, our political capital is our greatest asset. And yet we seem to have developed a reckless habit of all too freely lending it out. How have we—the group who has been doing emancipatory politics longer than any other people in this country— become so politically naïve and weak? Surely the Black church must accept its share of blame for that deplorable situation. The Black church cannot exist solely as a place where the community goes to experience a Sunday respite from the pressing burden of our people's history and present. As the preeminent institution for ADOS, Black churches in America must fill their sanctuaries with exhortations to carry out the sort of justice work that will relieve us of that burden! And insofar as mass movement politics threatens to generalize and oversimplify our struggle, then the Black church must seek to rescue our cause from being plunged into such a perilous amalgam. But where is a Black theology that can inform such a message? Where in the Bible can our people turn to find that which supports the clarion call now sounding for a new consciousness to be formed among ADOS, one that recognizes the primacy of building a specific political agenda around our needs before volunteering our advocacy in other causes that do not directly benefit us? How do we bring Black theology into closer alignment with the language of self-interest that (while it has fallen out of fashion as of late) has in fact traditionally been an essential feature in our group's political discourse?

In the next chapter, we will dig deeper into these questions and look at what the understanding of a singular Jewish identity meant to the group's political empowerment. Specifically, we will examine how the sin of Solomon—his prodigious desire for foreign women—was a rejection of the need for such a consciousness and how that rejection ultimately divided the kingdom of Israel and engendered great political turmoil. By looking at Solomon's capitulation to his many wives' requests that the gods they worshiped also be shown reverence in Jerusalem, we can observe the ways in which political alliances can function to encourage distraction from (and deterioration of) a necessary commitment to a specific people. That outcome, for ADOS, seems especially pronounced in the post-civil rights era, as it is during these intervening years when our leaders have most urged us to coalesce with other marginalized groups.

Chapter Two

Solomon

No Coalitions with the Mighty Until We've Lifted Weights

The temple that lay in ruins in Jerusalem, and to which Zerubbabel and the first wave of returnees had embarked from Babylon in order to rebuild, was originally constructed and dedicated to God by King Solomon in 966 BCE. During his reign, Solomon had taken a great number of foreign wives who were not of the Jewish faith. Doubtless he was looking to forge foreign alliances and expand the reach of the kingdom that his father, David, had ruled over (1 Kgs. 11:3). God had, however, expressly forbidden the king of Israel to enter into such unions, as it was foretold that by doing so the devotion in that regent's heart would surely be turned away from God (Deut. 17:17). If it was to be in accordance with God's covenant, these women would have had to convert to Judaism and thus disavow the practice of worshiping their gods. They would have had to adopt a way of life that respected the primacy of Jewishness and God's covenant with the community.

Solomon, however, did not compel these women to honor such a commitment. Instead, he built temples for all his wives in the holy city of Jerusalem so that they might venerate their gods with incense burning and sacrifice (1 Kgs. 11:7-8). He even participated in the worship of their gods. And as we read in 1 Kings 11:4, Solomon's devoutness to God indeed grew less and less, until there was nothing resembling the sort of stringent

17

and rigorous faithfulness that his father had once exhibited while he ruled over Israel. As punishment for this transgression, God plunged the kingdom of Israel into tumult; God fulfilled the earlier warnings that the kingdom would be divided and rendered vulnerable to foreign powers and that the great temple would be turned into a "heap of ruins" (1 Kgs. 9:8 NASB) because "[the Israelites] abandoned the LORD their God, who brought their ancestors out of Egypt" (v. 9 NLT).

The sin of Solomon and its implications for the viability of Israel (which, as a weak and fractured nation was forced into making alliances with Gentile nations whose interests did not advance the Jewish cause) suggest something germane for our purposes here as we explore a theology of ADOS. That is, when we think about the state of ADOS—and how our once vibrant movement, which was so tightly bound to a specific course of action for our people, but is now increasingly seen as being of a piece with other people's movements—hasn't our Black leadership in the post-civil rights era clearly transgressed in a manner so very similar to Solomon? Have our leaders not, in trying to realize their own political ambitions, made accommodations for other interests not unlike Solomon had? Have they not done this instead of working to ensure legislative gains for our people? And by unanchoring themselves from the legacy of our freedom struggle at a critical moment in the twentieth century, have they not left us to be so very vulnerable in coalition politics?

Indeed, just as Solomon took a great many foreign women for his spouses, so too have our Black leaders espoused many causes foreign to our own plight. And just as Solomon was observed to dramatically differ in his devotion to the Lord compared to his father, David, we can see how our leaders' hearts in relation to the hearts of our ancestors seem so estranged from our cause.

Today our leaders' minds appear evermore distant to the distinctiveness of our lineage and of all that we must fight and strive for because of it. In having wed our group to myriad people and their respective struggles—people whose places in the hierarchy naturally exceed ours as a racialized bottom caste—our leaders have greatly compromised our ability to be made whole. As civil rights icon Stokely Carmichael recognized, the relative weakness of American Descendants of Slavery in relation to other groups would perpetually dog our efforts in the pursuit of self-determination. Such alliances, Carmichael wrote in his classic text *Black Power: The Politics of Liberation*, "can seldom, if ever, be meaningful to the weaker partner."[1] And true to Carmichael's prediction, the subordination of ADOS interests within a coalition of diverse groups has been a hallmark of late twentieth- and twenty-first-century movement politics.

We need only consider the tremendous legislative gains and federal protections secured by the LGBTQ community in recent years—along with the gains and protections that have been conferred upon the country's immigrant population—to gain a sense of how the ADOS struggle functions as a crucial but ultimately disposable component of their campaigns of inclusion. Both the LGBTQ and immigrant rights movements have a history of appealing to figures from within the Black freedom struggle in America in order to lend their own causes a certain cachet and to rally public sentiment behind their efforts at inclusion. Gary Rivlin, a journalist at the *Chicago Reader* who had covered the bourgeoning Latinx movement in Chicago during the late 1980s, commented on this phenomenon when he said, "Black Chicago made a critical contribution to the Latino empowerment movement, both practically and spiritually. Latinos running [for office] on hopes and dreams and seemingly little else were inspired by the black experience."[2] No doubt ours is a profound and extraordinary cause. And it contains such great inspiration precisely because of the sheer scope of exclusion that our group has been up against. However, we still have such a long way to go. And our coalition partners seem to meet this latter truth with some skepticism.

In the case of Chicago in the late 1980s—a time when our group had just begun making some slow and long-delayed socioeconomic gains—there was an attitude prevalent among some of the city's Latino activists that seemed to suggest we had reached a kind of summit. Or, if not a summit, then at least a foothold comfortably far enough away from the reach of white supremacy. For the article

"The Blacks and Browns: Is the Coalition Coming Apart?" Rivlin interviewed Jesús García, who articulated this sentiment that the Black community had arrived: "Some of our frustrations stem from the fact that ... we're not yet as effective in the political arena as blacks are," García said. "We want to move ahead as fast as the black community is, but we haven't been involved as long." It is of course obvious that in 1987, minorities had not "been involved as long" as ADOS in the political struggle for inclusion. ADOS had, at that point, been engaged in the fight for over a century. What the Latino community lacked in experience, however, they more than made up for in how decisive their vote would prove to the Democratic Party. Recognizing that opportunity, García went on to say that the Latino community "need[s] to develop a municipal Latino agenda so that we can articulate our desires beyond more jobs or more contracts." In other words, the Latino community—while being part of a coalition with Blacks—needed to be extremely specific about who they were and what their needs were, and then go about placing demands on elected officials to deliver accordingly. Nathaniel Clay, who was the editor of the Black weekly *Chicago Metro News*, observed how "coalition politics, in this instance [were] simply a convenient cloak for ethnic ambitions."[3]

And indeed, to look at the breakdown between Latinos and Blacks in Chicago today, it is apparent how imbalanced these alliances can be (and often are). While Latinos were the poorest group in Chicago in the 1980s, they have since steadily outpaced Blacks. According to a 2017 report, only one-third of Blacks own a home in Chicago, compared to a little more than 40 percent of Latinos who are homeowners. In median household income, Latinos outperform Blacks $41,188 to $30,303. Unemployment in the Black community stands at 21 percent, while for Latinos it is less than 10 percent. And lastly, among households with zero net worth, Blacks make up 33 percent while Latinos are 27 percent.[4] That disparity in Chicago is part of a larger, national pattern that arguably reflects a preying upon ADOS disadvantage within minority coalitions. And while the ADOS individual's hope of liberation naturally increases as our group's struggle is incorporated into a larger, more formidable bloc, the lack of actual power possessed by our group necessarily diminishes our chances of that hope ever being realized. For too long now this inverse relationship between expectation and realization—between the input of our political energy and the outcome of our lived, material existence—has defined ADOS political engagement. No longer can this arrangement continue. As Carmichael perceived, it is necessarily the case that until we can leverage something to our advantage, our relative weakness will always render our struggle a mere accessory to the stronger group.

Our leadership must support our specific justice claim of reparations and empower us to pursue it; they cannot simply capitulate to political pressure to align with a less ADOS significant cause if it means furthering their career. Just as Solomon's sin and ancient Israel's manifold alliances with the Gentile nations resulted in one of the most tragic casualties of the kingdom—the children no longer speaking the language of Judah (Neh. 13:24)—it naturally will follow that with our leaders' hearts and minds aligned with causes that promise no change in our own economic position, our children's mouths will no longer speak the language of justice specific to the Black freedom struggle. Consider again the words of Stokely Carmichael: "Let black people organize themselves first," he wrote, "define their interests and goals, and then see what kinds of allies are available. Let any ghetto group contemplating coalition be so tightly organized, so strong, that—in the words of Saul Alinsky—it is an 'indigestible body' which cannot be absorbed or swallowed up."[5] Where today in the contemporary discourse of Black liberation do we hear that kind of unapologetic assertion of self-interest? It is rare if not entirely absent. Instead, we are made to speak in pagan tongues. The language of universal struggle has supplanted that of the singularity of the Black struggle. The language of doctrinaire Leftism would have us understand our particular struggle as inseparable from that of the American white working class (a group who has, throughout its entire history, so enjoyed a distinct advantage at the expense of ADOS). We are encouraged to speak the language of intersectionality, which would have us understand that the men of our race—those principal victims of white supremacy—are accorded some apparent privilege by virtue of their gender. How efficiently America continues to warehouse our most "privileged" in cages en masse! And of course, if today we voice our struggle, we must include other people of color. Failing this, we violate some sacrosanct principle of solidarity that casts our lot in with that of other marginalized communities despite the very real differences between them.

What are the implications of this erasure of our group's speech on future generations? So many of our ADOS children today do not speak our ancestors' language of justice. Surely future ADOS generations, too, will be lured into the worshiping of other groups' gods, of *their* inclusion, of *their* advantage in America. And in so doing they will have their hearts turned away from our cause. We will continue to lose sight of our own group's continued exclusion and our enduring and singular economic disadvantage, which if we are ever to participate as equals in these coalitions is the essential thing that we must ensure is remedied. Let us build ourselves and our institutions first. Let us remember all that was stolen from our ancestors in America so that we can recoup the resources we need in order to foster and retain our most talented instead of having our best and brightest simply be swept up into empire's supply chain of white supremacy production. After all, what better way to discretely ensure the dominance of supremacist ideology than to install a few people from the oppressed group in positions of influence? This creates the impression of diversity and progress while, at the same time, it perpetuates the subjugation of the group at large.

In the next chapter we will explore how, prior to the return of the exiles to Jerusalem, the Babylonian and Persian empires had pursued exactly this strategy of extraction of Jewish leaders through their deportation policies. The empires ensured a complete dearth of authentic Jewish servant-leaders who might have effectively mobilized the masses in Jerusalem to rebuild their city and community. We will see how these same conditions have been (and continue to be) present for ADOS in the United States.

Chapter Three

Daniel

Put on Ethnic Armor and Reject the Illusion of Inclusion

Among the Jewish elites who were deported to Babylon and their descendants, there were those who remained steadfast in their understanding of the Jews as a specific people. Of these patriots there was perhaps no better example than Daniel, for despite the Babylonian cultural milieu in which he was placed, Daniel remained single-mindedly committed to the preservation of Jewish heritage. He sought to live his life in a way that affirmed his identity as a Jew, even if it necessitated dissent.

When the king of Babylon attempted to get Daniel to change his kosher diet to conform with that of the Babylonians, he adamantly refused and "made up his mind to eat and drink only what God had approved for his people" (Dan. 1:8 CEV). Later, when the king of Medes issued his decree that called for a thirty-day moratorium on prayer, Daniel prayed in defiance three times daily with his window open toward Jerusalem. And although he was a privileged Jew in Babylon, which was located eight hundred miles away from the capital of the Jewish world, his prayers reflected a burden that he felt for his people who remained there languishing in poverty. Daniel's act of resistance, of course, led him to be sent to the lions' den, where he nonetheless remained unwaveringly faithful to God.

There was, in other words, nothing accidental or incidental (to borrow Dyson's terminology) about Daniel's Jewishness and his mindset about who he was and to which tribe he belonged. He recognized a vital truth: that it is impossible to make a difference *if you are not different*. If Israel is to be what God called the Jewish people to be, then Daniel perceived that the fulfillment of that promise depended on the Hebrew people's recognition of their being different from other people and other nations. That distinctiveness was set down through the laws and statutes of Yahweh, which were delivered to the Israelites through Moses. As long as they observed those laws, they were then able to maintain their uniqueness as a people.

To do this, of course, is particularly challenging when you are part of a society such as we discussed in the previous chapter: a society that makes no accommodations for such uniqueness, a society that rewards cultural conformity and threatens you with the fate of the lions' den and fiery furnaces should you not adhere to its norms and mores. That is why "accidental" Jews in Babylon would never have been in a position to be sent to the lions' den in the first place! What commitments to a specific group or cause could ever be possessed by individuals who understood themselves as being accidental members of that group? Any convictions they possessed, if they possessed any at all, could be easily cast off and discarded at the first sign that upholding them might present personal difficulties. And while an "incidental" Jew might have felt a kind of commitment to his or her oppressed group, he or she would no doubt also be keeping in mind all the many groups that were also oppressed in their own ways. For ADOS individuals, this might mean that they assign equal importance to the struggle of the white-led Me Too movement, or the LGBTQ community, or—as is becoming more common in our current moment—the immigrant community.

ADOS theology recognizes the plights and the experiences of these groups; and pastors must of course welcome them into our worship spaces and respect their identities in a way that accords with Christ's teaching. What ADOS theology strives for above all, however, is to highlight the necessity of ADOS *intentionally* identifying as ADOS before any other aspect of their identity. This deliberate identification is needed to cultivate the kind of "ethnic armor" that we observe in Daniel, who was so intentional in his identification as a Jew. That armor never allowed Babylon to bleach Jerusalem and his Jewish identity out of his consciousness. One of the great prayers that a Jew who had been deported to Babylon would recite is: "If I forget thee, O Jerusalem, let my right hand forget her cunning. If I do not remember thee, let my tongue cleave to the roof of my mouth" (Ps. 137:5–6 KJV). These words highlight the Jewish people's recognition of the necessity of guarding against the loss of their cultural distinctiveness and the hopelessness that surely awaits them if they do not. What good is my voice, the speaker of the prayer asks; toward what use should I put my hands if I do not privilege the communication and the expression of the specific history, traditions, and circumstances that have so uniquely shaped my people? The consequences of being severed from that connection are so grave, the prayer suggests, that the alternative of being rendered mute and handicapped is not only preferable but in fact deserved.

For ADOS, there must be a strong knowledge and celebration of self in relation to our historical experience. And at moments when it would be personally advantageous to renounce our place in that collective experience, or when it would be easier to pretend that we do not live every day in a society that is intent on reminding us of our subordinate place, it is then when it is most urgent to be suited with this ethnic armor. One such moment in my life occurred not long ago. It was nighttime and my wife, Barnetta, and I were driving home after a meal out. At the corner of Twenty-Second Street and Muhammed Ali Boulevard in downtown Louisville, police pulled us over. In my car's rearview mirror, tinted red and blue by the patrol car's lights, I saw reflected a deplorably routine sight for the Black motorist in America: two police officers exiting their cruisers and approaching the rear of my vehicle.

My wife and I were both at a total loss to identify what reason the officers had for initiating the stop. Perhaps in hindsight it is curious that we were so bewildered. After all, to be Black and inside a vehicle today, it seems, is to always be anticipating detainment in your journey. And more than just a basic inconvenience, a traffic stop for a Black person in America—regardless of one's complicity throughout the ordeal—is statistically shown to be a more terminal affair than for any other race or ethnicity. A menacing quality attends these roadside incidents, and as the beams from the officers' flashlights flooded my car, the bafflement that my wife and I were experiencing was accompanied by an acute sense of unease. Having my phone with me at the time, I took it out and began recording.

The area of Louisville in which the police officers had pulled us over was a poor, Black neighborhood. As a city that served as the national model for redlining, Louisville's landscape—particularly its western portion—is shamefully typified by the presence of these neighborhoods. They endure as part of the legacy of injustice and deliberate exclusion that has so profoundly shaped not just Black Louisville, but Black America at large. In such a part of town, my car, which was an Audi, must have appeared out of place to the officers. Perhaps that prompted them to feel that by stopping me, they would discover some other kind of criminal activity taking place, perhaps the solicitation of drugs or prostitution. Maybe they felt that there was a good chance that—whoever the driver of this car was—there was a warrant out for his arrest.

When one of the patrolmen appeared beside my window, he ordered me to keep my hands where he could see them. And before requesting to see the driver's licenses of both myself and my wife (a rather unusual and excessive demand, it seemed), the white police officer asked, in an arrogant and supercilious tone, "What're y'all getting into tonight?"

After verifying our identities and the proof of insurance on the vehicle, the officer told us that we were free to go. In what I suppose was an act of clemency, he relayed to my wife and me that we were being let off with "just a warning." At no time during the traffic stop did this officer feel it necessary to inform us as to *why* we had been pulled over. When I asked that he provide a reason, he replied that I had made an improper turn, although he admitted that he wasn't exactly sure what street it was off of. The officer then proceeded to tell me that the plastic frame around my license plate (which was something the dealership had put on the car when I purchased it) was illegal. Such flimsy reasoning only served to confirm what Barnetta and I had already suspected: that these two officers of the Louisville Metro Police Department had targeted us because we were Black, and that their pulling us over was in accordance with a pattern of hyper-policing of the Black community in which we are disproportionately targeted for these sort of investigatory stops that seek to increase arrest numbers in order to justify inflated police budgets. This approach of policing is, of course, not just unique to West Louisville; nor is the harassment of Black people by law enforcement a recent phenomenon. The suffering of such abuse has beset the Black community going back centuries. And so, following my own involvement with racist policing, the decision with which I was presented was whether I would simply be a passive victim of this disgraceful trend or if I would use the video documentation I had of my incident to shine a light on what was a patent example of discrimination and mistreatment, and a violation of police protocol.

There were, to be sure, a few factors discouraging the later choice. Not least among these was a concern that if I publicized my encounter, potential donorship to Simmons College—the institution of which I am the president—might dry up in response. And while the incident was certainly degrading and vexing, perhaps I could justify remaining silent about the confrontation since no physical harm had come to me or my wife, and we arrived home safely that night. Maybe the most prudent thing to do, I thought, would be to just forget about it. I could get on with my life, and by remaining quiet about the issue, I would not invite any hostilities that might compromise my ability to continue to effectively serve the community of West Louisville.

But therein lies exactly the issue that animates this chapter: what does it mean to effectively and authentically identify with, and serve, the community to which one belongs? In this particular instance, it became apparent that whatever I personally stood to lose by releasing the tape of my encounter with the police that night (whether it be the fraying of certain professional relationships or the loss of some degree of privacy and security), to not disclose the video tape would mean doing a disservice to the community. Any loss I might incur, I reasoned, would be a small price to pay if it led to meaningful action being taken against the foul custom of law enforcement deliberately targeting Black people under the assumption that they are doing something illegal. Moreover, my encounter with the police would lay bare the persistent myth that by meeting the supposed criteria for respectability in American society, a Black person might somehow transcend being recognized as something other than criminal, that by climbing the social ladder we will somehow find ourselves exempt from such crude and racist dealings with the police, or with society in general.

With these imperatives in mind, I decided to release the recording. It received nearly a hundred thousand views around the world. Subsequently, at St. Stephen Church a forum on racial profiling was convened in our Family Life Center. Attendance was at full capacity, a testament to how resonant and impactful the issue is within the community of West Louisville. Beyond the forum, prominent figures from within the city's clergy, both black and white, used the opportunity of my traffic stop to speak directly to the public about the bane of racial profiling and police bias.

Nevertheless, for all the support and productive discussion the matter generated, there was a predictable wave of criticism that sought to attribute certain self-aggrandizing motives to my disclosing the footage of my detainment. But for each negative accusation that was leveled at me, and for every assumption about my motivation that was being published and disseminated, the conviction I felt in my decision was only strengthened. These things only affirmed what I take to be a fundamental aspect of leadership and service to the community; that is, those who—like myself—are fortunate enough to be in positions of influence must be willing to make whatever sacrifices are called for in order to meaningfully advance the rest of our people.

Following my detainment, a wealthy and prominent Jewish friend contacted me. "Your real mistake was not that you were driving a luxury car through a poor, urban neighborhood," she said, "but that you were driving a German car." I was taken by how clearly and concisely that statement expressed her worldview. It showed just how powerfully shaped by the Jewish experience her interpretation of reality was. Here was someone who had obviously been educated to see all things in relation to her group's history, to overlay that lens of group identity and the plight of the Jews onto each situation and to have that inform and guide her understanding. And although my friend was sympathetic to Black pain, what was most consequential was her own ancestors' experience of suffering and the role the Germans played in it. From her perspective, the most damnable thing a Jew could do would be to drive a German car.

That level of self-awareness that she had as a Jew, resulting from the durability of memory and the deliberate choice to preserve it, is what a political education of a minority group living inside a dominant culture ought to be about. From the time of their captivity in Egypt (and particularly during their exile in Babylon), the Jewish people lived in climates that were naturally hostile to the development and preservation of a strong group consciousness. Yet they have always nurtured their cultural memory and sought to instill it throughout their group. In this way, there are certain resonances and significances with members of the ADOS community. Today, in a climate similar to Babylon, ADOS leadership must similarly resist the incentivized dissolution of our identity. We must eschew the trappings of a dominant culture that rewards conformity and silence. We must instead work to preserve the memory of all that has preceded us as a captive community and actively cultivate the potential to be a self-determinative people. As ADOS leaders, we cannot succumb to the temptation to trade in the awareness of our specific experience as a people and the fact that our oppression continues to be felt so vividly today. For what do we stand to gain by trading in that awareness? An always contingent place of influence? Feeling an always false sense of progress? The cold comfort of living with the *illusion of inclusion*? How long until that fraudulence finally overwhelms us? How very tragic for our people if it doesn't!

Chapter Four

Cyrus's Decree

No Liberation without Reparation

W hen Cyrus the Great conquered Babylon in 539 BC, he demonstrated a uniquely liberal spirit toward the Jews who were in captivity. It was he who had sent Zerubbabel to lead the first contingent of exiles back to Jerusalem in order to rebuild the temple, even financing the return through a taxation of Persian citizens. Cyrus also ordered that all of the gold and silver that had been stolen by Nebuchadnezzar II during the siege of Jerusalem in 597 BC be restored (Ezra 1:7).

Already we have discussed how the Samaritans—the "enemies of Judah" (Ezra 4:1)—sought to undermine the returning exiles' efforts with overtures of solidarity. But when the Samaritans' offer to participate in rebuilding the temple was explicitly rejected, Judah's enemies realized the futility of any efforts to form alliances that would ultimately function to neutralize the threat that the Jews posed to their dominion in the territory. The adversaries then turned to more overt means by which they could sabotage the work being done on the temple. Throughout the reigns of two separate rulers of the Persian Empire, the Samaritans were determined to carry out a campaign of disruption. They employed tactics intended to instill fear in the workers. They even sought out corrupt officials with bribes so that they might interrupt the progress that was being made (Ezra 4:4–5). Nonetheless, just as the subtle method of faux solidarity had not prevented the people from rebuilding the temple, neither did this sensational method of creating a climate of ridicule (along with attempts to grease the palms of certain officials) produce the desired results.

But if the Samaritans' initial efforts were subtle and their subsequent efforts more sensational in nature, then their last efforts were the most sinister. During the reign of Artaxerxes, they accused Zerubbabel of treason, alleging in a complaint to the king that Zerubbabel and the people of Jerusalem were going beyond what Cyrus had initially ordered (that is, only the rebuilding of the temple). They claimed that the people were also engaged in the rebuilding of the "rebellious and wicked" city of Jerusalem and the surrounding wall (Ezra 4:12). They maintained that the consequences of the people finishing their work would economically disempower the empire. Alas, this method was the one that finally proved successful. The king immediately responded with an order for the Samaritans to go and ensure the discontinuation of the work that was occurring in Jerusalem.

And so they did. The work ceased, and the people of Jerusalem were dispirited in the face of sustained Samaritan antagonism. The work on the temple was not renewed until years later, after the prophets Haggai and Zechariah began to exhort the people of Jerusalem to engage in civil disobedience and defy the stop work order. This mobilization of the people, however, was not easy. In Haggai 1:2 we read how the people had expressed skepticism about whether it was the right time to begin rebuilding the temple. Some of those who had returned with Zerubbabel, we are told, had in fact turned their attention to building their *own* houses. Through Haggai, God enjoined them to consider what such self-interest had produced in the way of uplift for the people as a whole (Haggai 1:5–9). Indeed, while they had prioritized themselves, they had neglected the service demanded by God. As a result, the people lacked for sufficient resources with which they could meet their basic needs. Haggai admonished them and—fearful of further punishment by God—the people were stirred to collective action and again began to work on rebuilding the temple.

Again, however, the opponents of the Jews sought to intervene. They confronted the workers and demanded to know by whom they had been authorized to lay the foundation of the temple. Zerubbabel informed them that it was by decree of King Cyrus that the work they were doing was to be completed. Also, Zerubbabel told them that Cyrus had additionally ordered the officials to restore the possessions that had originally been stolen from the Jews. And so the local officials sent word to Darius I—the king at the time—to make inquiry into the royal treasury archives in Babylon to corroborate Zerubbabel's and the elders' claims. At the citadel of Ecbatana, Darius located the scrolls that delineated the work that was to be done on the temple. He responded to the officials who had sent him the letter, and in his response he reinstituted Cyrus's initial decree and again pledged funds from the government to see the project through to completion. "Moreover, I hereby decree what you are to do for these elders of the Jews in the construction of this house of God: Their expenses are to be fully paid out of the royal treasury, from the revenues of the Trans-Euphrates, so that the work will not stop" (Ezra 6:8 NIV).

What Darius finds in Cyrus's decree—and what ultimately allows for the restoration and dedication of the temple—is something that is foundational to ADOS theology—namely, that there is no liberation without reparation. There is no _justice_ without reparation. This is one of the gospel's most vivid and concrete truths, and throughout our reading of the Bible we encounter it time and time again. In Genesis 15:13–14 (NIV), God says to Abram, "Know for certain that for four hundred years your descendants will be strangers in a country not their own and that they will be enslaved and mistreated there. But I will punish the nation that enslaves them, _afterward they will come away with great possessions_" (emphasis mine). In Exodus 3:21–22 (NLT), the promise that God made to Abram is reemphasized to Moses four hundred years later: "And I will cause the Egyptians to look favorably on you. They will give you gifts when you go so you will not leave empty-handed." And in what is surely the gospel's most explicit instance of reparations, Luke 19:8–9 (GNT) tells how Zacchaeus stood up before the Lord and said, "Listen, sir! I will give half my belongings to the poor, and if I have cheated anyone, I will pay back four times as much." In a testament to the primacy of monetary reparations when making meaningful atonement for wrongs committed, Jesus responded to Zacchaeus, "Salvation has come to this house today." Indeed, if America is to meaningfully atone for its moral and economic transgressions against ADOS through slavery and the discrimination beyond, then salvation must come through policy that redistributes wealth specifically to our group. Government intervention—exactly of the sort that we see Cyrus effect for the rehabilitation of Jerusalem—is key to ADOS beginning our healing, our restoration. When Ezra leads a second delegation of exiles from Babylon back to Jerusalem in 443 BC during the reign of Artaxerxes I, the king also provides Ezra with wealth (Ezra 7:15). We even read how, if that money were to prove insufficient, Ezra was to be given whatever resources would be necessary from the royal treasury.

Capital—particularly the capital that would otherwise be available had it not been stolen—is of course an indispensable component of a broken people's ability to adequately reconstruct themselves. But in terms of priority, the need for those people to receive an education about what was done to them to make them so broken in the first place, to help impress upon them the specificity of who they are as a people and why they must bear that specificity in mind before, during, and after they rebuild, is absolutely paramount. In the next chapter, we will become more acquainted with Ezra, another Jew who was living in exile in Babylon. Ezra was a "scribe skilled in the law of Moses" (Ezra 7:6), which as we know stipulated the essential customs and practices that the Jewish community was to observe in honor of their distinction in God's eyes. The law of Moses is what made them unique; it served as the foundation for a way of being in the world both religiously and politically. What we will see is how, following the rebuilding of the temple in Jerusalem by Zerubbabel and the elders, many of the people had strayed from adhering to the principles and customs required to maintain their uniqueness. And in much the same way that Ezra returned to Jerusalem intent on reinstilling God's laws and regulations—to urge the people toward a consciousness of and commitment to who they were as a specific people—we will see how this lineage-focused pedagogical mission is foundational to the leaders of the ADOS movement as well.

Chapter Five

Ezra

Lineage Alone as a Call to Specificity for ADOS's Unique Justice Claim

W hen Ezra arrived in Jerusalem in 456 BCE, it was with great dismay that he realized how the people there had become so lapsed in their devotion to God and the edicts set down in the covenant. Among the impieties to which Ezra bore witness, the one that most shocked his conscience was the intermarriages that had occurred between the Jews and the foreign tribes (Ezra 9:1–2). As we discussed in chapter 2, these unions were prohibited by God because they would lead the Jewish people into worshiping pagan deities, thus compromising the necessary preservation of tribal cohesion. Importantly, Ezra reports that it was the leaders in the Jewish community who had set a precedent in this manner (Ezra 9:1). The priests and Levites (religious functionaries with special privileges and duties associated with temple service) had taken wives from the neighboring tribes, neglecting their devotion to God in favor of greater socioeconomic mobility through marrying members of the more affluent surrounding communities.

And so, with a corrupt leadership engaging in the sort of inter-marriages that would lead to cultural disintegration, the people were naturally led astray as well. A distraught Ezra prayed and lamented over the sin of intermarriage and the implications of assimilation on Jewish identity and their future as a group. God had commanded that they were "never [to] seek their peace or prosperity" by forming alliances with them (Ezra 9:12). Ezra's lamentations moved the people to repent of their misdeed, and he used the power of regional governance with which Artaxerxes I had invested him to annul the marriages. He then proclaimed that all the returned exiles were to come to Jerusalem within three days; if they did not, they would forfeit their property and be expelled from the Jewish community.

Here again we see the primacy of determining who is to be included and who is to be excluded in the project of reconstituting the community. In order to recall to the exiles the singularity of their experience and their unique place in God's plan, Ezra emphasized how it was lineage and *lineage alone* that conferred rightful belonging in the Jewish covenant community. In Ezra 2, he provides an extensive list of about forty thousand names of Jews whose lineages all trace back to the deportation from Jerusalem by Nebuchadnezzar. It is through this lens of lineage that Ezra preaches the covenant established between God and the chosen people. Indeed, one of the most powerful images that we come across later, in the book of Nehemiah, is when Ezra is standing on a platform at the Water Gate in Jerusalem to address the newly tribalized, newly *conscious* Israelites. There, from dawn until noon, Ezra reads the "statutes and rules" of the Law of the Lord to those who had gathered. Critically, we are told that the platform on which Ezra stood was one that "[the people] had made for the purpose" (Neh. 8:4 KJV).

In other words, the message of Jewish specificity that was being delivered *to* the people was being delivered to them from a platform made *by* those very people. Thinking about the situation that confronts ADOS today in terms of our renewal and our restoration as a people, is that not the very inverse of our situation? We must ask ourselves: From where can our leaders address the ADOS community with messages capable of resonating so deeply and so completely with our experience of oppression and our unique struggle? MSNBC? CNN? Given those networks' corporate agendas, that hardly seems likely. Their interests, it is evident, lie in maintaining the status quo. And that status quo is one in which ADOS, after four hundred years, still find ourselves lodged beneath a great many other groups as a permanent bottom caste. Can we really be surprised when these platforms yield us nothing in the way of escaping our continued oppression? How—when our people did not build them for that purpose—could they do otherwise? Being as they are not sustained by ADOS, it would seem the very height of fantasy for us to believe that we could ever derive any real power from them.

The cynical among us will say that the politicians are too corrupt or the country too constitutionally racist to ever permit a space for ADOS to exercise such self-determination. And however cynical such pronouncements are, it must be conceded that there is a measure of real, undeniable truth to them. Verily, we would search in vain for a moment in our history when America has not made clear its lack of appetite for our group's progress. And yet it must be recognized that those times where we have made inroads into securing the rights and privileges that are supposed to attend citizenship in America were times when our sense of ourselves as a *specific group* was at its strongest. These were times when our leaders recognized the primacy of our specific needs! And like the returnees in Jerusalem whose (mis)leadership had adulterated their identity, so too has our modern leadership class led us down a path that promises only to further fracture our identity. Their attitudes and behaviors only aid America in her innate and unique antagonisms against our group. White supremacy is strongest in defending against our justice claim when our sense of ourselves and our commitments are scattered and unfocused. Our leaders have failed to bear in mind the centrality of our lineage. And rather than foregrounding that factor in *affirming* justice for our group, they have instead abetted America in its efforts to redefine our group in order to *deny* us our due justice.

The redefinition of Blackness in America finds its genesis in the 1965 Hart-Celler Immigration and Naturalization Act (INA). It was at this time when—instead of Blackness being most appropriately understood by looking at the specific economic consequences of skin being fixed in a person's lineage—Blackness began to be identified with a person's color. The INA promoted this diluted understanding of Blackness by emphasizing family reunification and the importation of skilled immigrant labor, a marked departure from the aims of preceding immigration policy. It abolished the nationality-based quota system that had, up to that point, shown clear preference for admitting immigrants from European (which is to say *white*) nations. The new amendments instead encouraged an inflow of immigrants from African countries and the Caribbean, helping to significantly alter the composition of Black America in the latter part of the twentieth century. For instance, at the outset of the new policy, foreign-born Blacks had made up just 1.8 percent of the total Black population in the United States. However, with these new criteria in place, that percentage would rise to 3.1 by the year 1980.[1]

Subsequent policy would only continue that upward trend. That very same year, a new piece of immigration reform—the Refugee Act of 1980—would further promote the resettlement of foreign-born Blacks in America as it lifted the annual limit of accepting persons fleeing civil and international conflicts from 17,500 to 50,000.[2] This act introduced a new wave of immigrants from African countries (particularly from the continent's horn region, which was then mired in strife) and an influx of Haitians who were coming to the United States hoping to be granted asylum. A decade later, the 1990 Immigration Act's diversity visa program would provide yet another avenue for Africans looking to immigrate to the United States. Importantly, as demographer Arun Peter Lobo points out in his paper "U.S. Diversity Visas are Attracting Africa's Best and Brightest," one salient feature of this pool of African immigrants was its particular class character. "[B]ecause African immigrants are disproportionately in professional, managerial, and technical (PMT) occupations," Lobo writes, "[. . .] their departure could further undermine social and economic conditions on the African continent."[3] Diversity immigrants, in other words, tend to be well-educated and highly skilled. And while Lobo is certainly right to point out the implications of the loss of human capital on the African continent, it must also be said that the potential for undermining certain social and economic conditions is not restricted to one end of the African immigrant's journey. Indeed, when our country annually receives tens of thousands of Black people who don't come out of our group's unique experience of economic oppression (and who thus necessarily possess a distinct advantage over our group in navigating American life), how can such a thing not work to reinforce white society's perception that Black people in America aren't held back by the legacy of chattel slavery? "Why just look," these people might say, "there are plenty of Black men and women here in America who appear to be doing just fine for themselves! How can you ADOS realistically claim that racism is preventing you from achieving anything?"

Society is eager to paper over certain distinctions that necessarily inhere in the Black experience(s) in America. And that is arguably because dealing with our group's specific experience demands accountability and a massive redistribution of wealth that was stolen from us. It is no wonder that rather than make any effort to provide restitution for our group's experience of oppression, the government instead passes immigration policy that merely supports the melting pot mythos of America, one which today yields an increasingly homogenized Blackness from which our group does not materially benefit. No, for purposes of authentic justice, ADOS must be recognized by our unique designation. We must begin to focus on what ADOS life actually looks like when our group is parceled out from other "people of color," a catchall that necessarily encompasses a more economically diverse group of people, and which is so detrimental to our justice claim. The project of ADOS is a call to specificity not unlike the one that Ezra issued when he returned to Jerusalem. Our project is one of how we organize ourselves politically to advocate most meaningfully for the US government to make good on the unpaid debt to our group—for slavery, Jim Crow, and its 124-year commitment to denying ADOS the promise initially set down in the *Plessy v. Ferguson* ruling. Our project is asserting that only we—by virtue of our lineage and our lived experience—get to make that demand and that outside groups do not have the latitude to intervene in our affairs and opine on how that redistribution is managed.

The next chapter will take the *Plessy v. Ferguson* decision (and how its "separate but equal" ruling was so egregiously mishandled) as a catalyst for a discussion on the necessity of reparations. Moreover, we will interrogate a deep theological divide as it pertains to the very concept of reparations. In so doing, we will uncover the ways in which any form of recompense that does not directly attend to the precarity of ADOS institutions is something that will ultimately ensure the continuity of the *Plessy v. Ferguson* misimplementation and its legacy of failing to produce its stated aim of equity in our community.

Chapter Six

Esau

A Good Lesson from a Bad Example

The Supreme Court's decision in the 1896 *Plessy v. Ferguson* case declared "separate but equal" to be America's official racial policy. But while ADOS were indeed made to exist separately from white society, America never delivered on its promise to make our spaces equal to those of their white counterparts. Public schools, for example, were one area where the misimplementation of the separate but equal doctrine was glaringly obvious. This phenomenon was documented in great detail by a young Howard University law student named Thurgood Marshall. Along with his teacher Charles Hamilton Houston, Marshall traveled throughout the US South in the early 1930s, documenting the sharp disparity in resource allocation among ADOS and white schools. Together, Houston and Marshall brought their findings to the NAACP, who filed a lawsuit against the US government for a violation of *Plessy v. Ferguson.*

The goal of Houston and Marshall was not to have the Supreme Court's separate but equal doctrine dismantled but rather to have it truly enforced. However, in response to this demand for equity, liberal Supreme Court Justice Earl Warren issued a statement that smacked of white supremacy: "Does segregation of children in public schools solely on the basis of race, even though the physical facilities and other 'tangible' factors may be equal, deprive the children of the minority group of equal educational opportunities?" Warren asked. "We believe that it does. We conclude that in the field of public education the doctrine of 'separate but equal' has no place. Separate educational facilities are inherently unequal."[1]

In Warren's statement it is difficult not to hear the insidious notion that anything which is predominantly Black has no value. The assumption is that white schools are superior just by virtue of their whiteness, and that—conversely—Black schools are inferior by virtue of their Blackness. Regrettably, this prejudice against ADOS institutions and businesses is one to which even our own people succumb. For instance, in West Louisville there is an ADOS-owned carwash. It has all the same equipment as the white-owned carwashes in town, but it takes much longer to get through. I recall once being at this carwash and hearing an ADOS customer in the lobby become impatient. "This is why I don't patronize Black businesses," he said, wryly shaking his head. It seemed that, almost instinctively, this man attributed the slow service to the Blackness of the facility. Similarly, I remember when a member of St. Stephen left our church to join a white megachurch in the more affluent suburbs. When I asked this person about the decision to leave, the response was that the white church offered more children's programs and the facilities were an improvement on those found at most Black churches. Like the individual whom I'd overheard at the carwash that day, the former member of our church appeared to ascribe an innate superiority—attributable to whiteness—when it came to the supposedly higher quality services and facilities found at the white church.

However, insofar as ADOS space is inferior to white space, that condition is neither inherent nor natural to the former. Rather, it is because our institutions have long been denied the resources that would allow them to operate to the best of their potential. They furthermore operate in and serve communities that have also been excluded from access to resources. This dynamic is something that many white liberals today fail to really grasp. And like former Justice Warren, they appear to believe that the ADOS community will best be served by diversifying predominantly white institutions. This belief informs their ideas about what our rehabilitation will entail, and oftentimes they are ideas that—because the control of the resources ultimately remain in white hands—promise nothing of the kind of actual institutional empowerment that ADOS people so desperately need for our liberation.

As an ADOS institution builder, I come up against this paternalistic attitude quite often. However, one incident in particular figures prominently in my memory. It was during the 2019 Angela Project Conference in Birmingham, Alabama, where I was facilitating a discussion on racial justice with the national faith community. While the presentations were being given, I received an email with a link to an article that had run in that day's *Courier-Journal*, a Kentucky-based newspaper. Initially entitled "Lining Louisville Rev. Kevin Cosby's Pockets with $9M Does Not Count for Reparations," the *Courier-Journal* l ater revised the headline to read "Giving Rev. Kevin Cosby's College $9M Does Not Count as Reparations." In either headline, the implication was clear: whatever might constitute justice for the ADOS community, it would not be up to those who bear the burden of that injustice to decide.

What had prompted the white journalist at the *Courier-Journal* to take to its pages and opine on the subject of reparations in the first place was Empower West's call for Louisville's Southern Baptist Theological Seminary to pay reparations to Simmons College, a request that I proudly and unapologetically signed. Empower West is a coalition of Black and white Louisville-area pastors who regularly convene to discuss matters of racial justice both at the local and national level. Through the power of education and spirituality, we work together to promote economic uplift among West Louisville residents. And so, after Southern Baptist Theological Seminary released a seventy-two-page study detailing just how vital chattel slavery had been to the institution from its very inception, we proposed that the seminary pay reparations to Simmons College. Such a gesture would, after all, be in keeping with the decree found in the report's opening statement, which was written by the Seminary's president. "We must repent of our own sins," R. Albert Mohler Jr. wrote.

"We cannot repent for the dead. We must offer full lament for a legacy we inherited."[2] But if Southern Seminary is being truly honest about that legacy that they have inherited, then isn't it more than just a racist legacy? More than just past attitudes and patterns of discrimination against ADOS? Have they not also inherited all the *wealth* that was stolen from ADOS by their racist ancestors as well?

Indeed, among the report's many revelations was how—with all of Southern Seminary's founders having been slaveholders—the institution's funding derived directly from the proceeds of exploited slave labor. Additionally, when Southern was later in jeopardy of closing, a member from its board of trustees—then-governor of Georgia Joseph Brown—interceded with a $50,000 check to rescue the institution from certain financial ruin. That gift, too, was packaged in sin. For it is widely known that Joseph Brown amassed his fortune in large part through the inhumane (yet legal) practice of convict leasing—that is, forced labor performed by Black men and children who had been arrested for the slightest of offenses. These men were routinely denied just hearings or due process and were given extremely punitive sentences to extend their servitude as convict laborers.[3] By its own admission, Southern was able to enrich itself through our people's stolen labor. Therefore, it seemed only appropriate that—with Simmons College being an institution that (like all historically Black colleges and universities [HBCUs]) was forced to exist in order to attend to the unique needs of the descendants of that historically excluded population—we request that Southern lead by radical Christian example and pay reparations to Simmons College.

The writer of the *Courier-Journal* article, however, evidently felt that Empower West's request for Southern to do what is right—to do what is necessary to help alleviate the burden borne by those in the West Louisville community because of the institution's past actions—ran afoul of some notion of what form racial healing is meant to take. From the article's opening paragraph, it recapitulated some of the most destructive assumptions and paternalistic attitudes that have done enormous damage to ADOS progress and ADOS aspiration. At root, the article is based on a flawed premise concerning ADOS institutions and the aim of ADOS self-determination: namely, that committing funding to a school like Simmons College (an institution which proudly reflects ADOS culture and centers ADOS concerns) signals something akin to a return to segregation. In the writer's eyes, when ADOS-governed institutions make that kind of specific commitment to serving their group, it can only result in a more segregated society.

The obvious question that presents itself, though, is whether we have ever truly left segregation. Even a cursory look at recent demographic data would indicate that we exist just as separately today as we did before. True, our cities and towns no longer enforce the partition of their white and Black populations. But we nonetheless find that—irrespective of income level—that process is more or less automated now anyway due to centuries of white hostility and intolerance to the idea of integration. HBCUs like Simmons College do not exist to promote segregation, as the *Courier-Journal* article appeared to suggest. Rather, as earlier stated, they exist *because* of it. Despite these institutions facing overwhelming challenges throughout that existence, HBCUs have nonetheless produced some of our nation's most outstanding leaders, from Martin Luther King Jr. to Thurgood Marshall. They have given us influential figures in the media like Oprah Winfrey and Spike Lee. In my hometown of Louisville I am surrounded by the success stories of HBCUs; local leaders like Darryl Owens, Jecorey Arthur, Gerard Neal, Walter Malone, Bruce Williams, school board member Corey Schull, and Metro Council leaders like Keisha Dorsey and Jessica Green are all products of these institutions. And when we look at the composition of the Black professional class in America today—business executives, federal judges, and doctors—we find that it is disproportionately made up of HBCU graduates. Fifty percent of all Black public-school teachers and school personnel come from HBCUs.[4] And to think: all this success, all this achievement, while representing only 3 percent of colleges in the whole of the United States. Even more impressive, all while working with such a stark deficit of resources as a result of the tremendous level of wealth theft from the ADOS community and the enduring legacy of anti-ADOS discrimination.

As an HBCU president, I deal with the devastating effects of this wealth gap firsthand every single day. I recognize it in students who cannot afford the cost of college, even a relatively modest one such as Simmons. I observe it in our staff and faculty who—because there simply are not enough resources at hand to hire additional and much-needed staff—are required to fulfill multiple roles. The racial wealth gap reveals itself when we, as an ADOS institution, find ourselves having difficulty maintaining old, dilapidated buildings while the more affluent schools can easily subsidize the construction of new stadiums and athletic fields. And it is precisely because so much of that wealth in white colleges and universities can be traced back to their complicity in practices that denied our ADOS ancestors' humanity, and exploited their labor, that public funding of HBCUs is considered by many experts to be a critical component of any reparations package.

In his written statement submitted to Congress's hearing on H.R. 40—the proposal to form a commission to study reparations—Dr. Sandy Darity, the nation's premiere scholar on the economics of restitution for ADOS, argued, "Some portion of funds could be devoted to community or institution-based purposes, for example, support for the historically black colleges and universities."[5] And while Dr. Darity would rightly emphasize that the collection and allocation of that money is the duty of the US government (since, owing to policy directly responsible for perpetuating wealth inequality, the wealth gap bears that particular entity's imprimatur quite conspicuously), when we talk about reparations in a *Christian* sense, then I cannot think of a more appropriate way for Southern Baptist Seminary to lead authentically than for that institution to pay reparations to Simmons College.

Indeed, so long as President Mohler and his board continue to hold onto their ill-gotten institutional wealth, they brazenly make a mockery of genuine Christian racial reconciliation. There is no doubt a special sort of hypocrisy in an institution like Southern that—on one hand—professes to use the Bible as its guide and ultimate source of moral authority, and yet—on the other—perpetuates the wretched sins of its forebears by not engaging in authentic Christian atonement. As we have read in President Mohler's response to Southern Seminary's crimes against humanity, he merely says that they "lament." But as anyone who is familiar with the teachings of Christ would know, lamentation is not the appropriate biblical response to sin. When we offend and transgress (and Southern has admittedly greatly transgressed), the Bible calls on us to *repent*.

In Scripture we are shown numerous examples of what form repentance—if it is to be authentic—is supposed to take. In Hebrews 12:17, we see the word *repent* being used in reference to Esau, who "despised his birthright" (Gen. 25:34). Esau lost his blessing of primogeniture because of a weakness of his character, but his repentance is important because there is a specific dimension to his sorrow in which he expresses his wish to have the effects of his past actions reversed. In this way, he is a good model for Southern Baptist Seminary in terms of what repentance must entail. Authentic repentance for personal enrichment at the expense of other people always demands an economic dimension. In Exodus 22:1, we are told that if you steal a person's livestock, you must reverse the effects of your crimes by paying restitution equaling four to five times as much as the value of what you stole. In 2 Samuel 12, David says a thief should pay back "four times" in reparations. And in Luke 19, Zacchaeus, who had enriched himself through graft, tells Jesus that he will restore to his victims four times more than he stole. It is in fact only after Zacchaeus promises to pay reparations that Jesus affirms that salvation has come to his house. And so when Empower West proposed that Southern Seminary pay reparations to Simmons College, we were making a moral plea for that institution to bring true salvation to their house and not merely offer a vain lament that is incompatible with the doctrine of Christianity and atonement they claim to embrace. As Southern Baptist conservative orthodox theologian A. H. Strong argues in his classic text, *Systematic Theology*, "True repentance is indeed manifested and evidenced by confession of sin before God *and by reparation for wrongs done to men*" (emphasis mine).[6]

When the *Courier* ran the column that sought to police how the distribution of wealth that had accrued at the expense of ADOS should be executed, the newspaper unwittingly highlighted a theological rift between two markedly divergent perspectives on the nature of the gospel and Christian faith. There are, in essence, two kinds of religion: formal religion and formative religion. Formal religion is best characterized as being vertically oriented; it is a piety that says the only role of religion is to connect the people with God. Traditional Christian evangelicals believe that this is what the church should strive for—simply save people's souls and secure their allegiance to Christ as their savior. Formative religion, on the other hand—while it recognizes the importance of the vertical dimension of religion—also orients itself horizontally. Contrasted against a monastic style of religious practice, formative religion seeks to engage with the world and take seriously the concerns of the oppressed. The reason that those founders of Southern Baptist Seminary could claim to be Christian while enslaving other human beings is because they only ever received and knew Jesus as their savior. They never followed him as Lord, because to do so would necessarily require a commitment to righting the injustices they perpetuated.

Today, those at Southern do not feel the need to address the economic injustice in which they are complicit because it falls outside the realm of formal religion. And while I of course believe that the church ought to evangelize so that people might receive Jesus as their savior, I also believe that after receiving him, Christians are then further called upon to follow Jesus as Lord. Because if following Jesus as savior influences one's vertical relationship with God, then when Jesus is known as Lord, it affects one's horizontal relationship with people and the world around him or her. In Matthew 23:37–39, Jesus clearly states, "Love the Lord thy God with all thy heart. . . . Thou shalt love thy neighbor as thyself" (KJV). I believe that what Jesus is communicating here in this edict is that while there is a dimension of Christian faith that is personal (that is, a relationship between oneself and God), the Christian faith is never private in the sense that there are no attendant concerns for our world and for others around us. God is not calling the church to a kind of monasticism detached from issues of racial and economic justice. Indeed, from an authentic Christian perspective, racism is much more than a sociological abnormality; it is a veritable doctrine of demonism. Racism is idolatry not only because it creates God in a white image but it also presumes to speak on the prerogatives of God by making whiteness something transcendent. Southern Seminary has, from its very inception, been bound up in this sinful relationship with idolatry, with demonism, and the pernicious effects of such a theology cannot be overstated. We have a segregated society in America today because we first had segregated churches that sanctioned and preached a segregated and racist theology. Before Blacks were devalued in society, they were devalued in these churches. Before "Whites Only" and "Colored Only" signs appeared in the public square to separate the races, they appeared in these worship spaces. All the things that have historically worked to keep Blacks as a bottom caste in America—from slavery to lynching, to convict leasing and segregation—were theologically justified by Southern Baptist theology. And when the *Courier-Journal* ran a column essentially chiding Empower West for proposing that Southern Seminary should provide recompense to a Black-led institution in a city that must wrestle every day with the effects of Southern's actions, the *Courier-Journal* sided with the transgressor and not the transgressed.

It is worth recalling the words of Martin Luther, who in "An Open Letter concerning the Hard Book against the Peasants" wrote, "One who lives in a community must do his share in bearing and suffering the community's burdens, dangers, and injuries, even though not he, but his neighbor, has caused them. He must do this in the same way that he enjoys the peace, profit, protection, wealth, freedom and convenience of the community, even though he has not won them or brought them into being."[7] Indeed, Southern must do its share in bearing the community's burdens, for its generational neighbors were responsible for so much suffering. It must do this in the same way it enjoys the wealth of its generational neighbors. The writer of the *Courier-Journal* article evidently felt that Empower West's request for Southern Seminary to recognize and carry out this civic duty (which is in fact also a very Christian duty) was beyond the pale. Instead, the writer argued that white colleges should liberalize their admissions policies and offer scholarships to promote increased enrollment of ADOS children into some of the "better schools." In addition to these sorts of reforms, the writer supported corporate mentoring programs that would help ADOS graduates better navigate the business world. Ultimately, however, these measures perpetuate the cycle of dependency on white institutions and white businesses. And if we are to break the cycle, what ADOS institutions require is the United States government making good on its original promise in the *Plessy v. Ferguson* ruling. What ADOS people need is for white liberals to support us in our call to go beyond strategies that avoid dealing with the accrued disadvantages that so inhibit our full participation in society. We must cease to rely solely on a smattering of philanthropists to pick up the tab for the ongoing catastrophic situation in the ADOS community. Since that catastrophe is one that was crafted through public policy that specifically disadvantaged us, its effects must be reversed through public policy that specifically advantages us. To the extent that the philanthropic arrangement continues to define efforts at promoting progress and development within the ADOS community, I believe all that will be promoted is still greater dependence. There will only be a deepening of longstanding assumptions about ADOS, assumptions held not only among so many white Americans but—even more tragically—among so many ADOS as well. For when ADOS-led institutions are struggling to survive in the absence of adequate resources, feelings about our group's supposed inferiority will invariably develop in the people whom those institutions are meant to serve and empower.

For the white donor class, ADOS institutions are perceived as simply too risky of an investment. It is the continuation of a tradition of exclusion that, in this form, might be called "philanthropic redlining." If redlining was the conscious decision by banks and insurance companies to undercapitalize ADOS communities by deciding that they would not be the recipients of government mortgages and loans, then philanthropic redlining is simply the natural extension of that project of exclusion. Now, however, the process is not so much conscious, or explicit, as it is simply automatized. Here in Louisville, nothing more clearly illustrates this phenomenon than the recent construction of a brand-new, multimillion-dollar YMCA in the city's west end. Funded by the collective philanthropic efforts of a local bank, various foundations, and a major international corporation, the new YMCA sits less than two miles from another recreational facility, the Family Life Center at St. Stephen Church. In some respects, there are striking similarities between the two facilities. Both the YMCA and St. Stephen Church have their roots in the Christian faith. They both provide a valuable civic service. Except for a swimming pool, the Family Life Center at St. Stephen is equipped with everything that one would find in the new YMCA. Both are classified as a 501(c) (3), or a tax-exempt, charitable organization. As such, these entities can incentivize individuals or businesses to contribute to them, since those donations will be entirely deductible on a tax return. However, the stories of how these two establishments came to fruition could not be more dissimilar. And comparing what our experience at St. Stephen entailed in terms of securing the funds necessary to build and sustain the Family Life Center to that of the new YMCA proves beyond a shadow of a doubt how powerfully the history of ADOS exclusion asserts itself in the present, and how it shapes the unequal outcomes that keep our community in such a state of want and hardship.

Prior to the YMCA's doors even being opened, a major corporation had already donated two million dollars to the venture. These monies would not only aid in the actual physical construction of the YMCA but also be used to subsidize memberships to those in the community. St. Stephen had no such enthusiastic, well-heeled backers when we set out to create a place where the community could come together and have access to programs intended to promote spiritual, mental, and bodily wellness. In the absence of those investors, we were forced to develop our facilities the hard way. We had to take out a loan and then undertake the work of motivating the people in the community and in the church to invest in the institution to ensure its success and longevity. Quite simply, the dynamics at play in the building of the new YMCA and the Family Life Center in Louisville offer a stark reflection of the basic distinction that has always determined the difference between white life and ADOS life: advantage and disadvantage. The boost and the block. A hand-up and a handicap. And because the government has given white America the former and left ADOS to deal with the latter, we lack the natural, beneficial associations that follow from belonging to a group in which advantage has been consolidated.

In the white community, those individuals who are looking to raise funds for their projects can leverage their connections in a way that ADOS simply have never been able to. And that is why the YMCA was funded so expediently as opposed to the Family Life Center—because every day we suffer the exclusion of the government and the assumptions of white society. There is little reason to suspect that government and philanthropy would have ever so eagerly supported a similar institutional vision led by ADOS, especially if it was a white institution that had already been in the community for several years the way that St. Stephen Church has been. But when I brought this opinion before leaders in the philanthropic community, they either quickly dismissed the charge or they believed that the ends justified the means, that because it would ultimately occasion economic activity within the community, then we could (and perhaps should) overlook the obvious discrepancies in who is actually leading these initiatives. The outcome, however, is always that whites maintain wealth advantage over ADOS.

Doubtless, the greatest tragedy with respect to the new YMCA is that the ADOS community already had a Y less than five miles away. From that facility's very beginning in 1914, the Black Chestnut Street YMCA has subsisted on ADOS dollars. It has sought to provide specifically for the community that it serves, establishing the Black Achievers scholarship program that, for decades, raised hundreds of thousands of dollars to provide college scholarships for Black youths in Louisville. It was also the venue for the annual Fathers and Sons banquet. Now, though, as the new upscale Y has been built—a project that was overseen by whites who are not part of the community—the Black Y on Chestnut Street is in total dilapidation. And in this outcome we see exemplified how racism operates in America today. The story of the two YMCAs in Louisville bears out the chilling prophesy of Benjamin Elijah Mays, the former president of Morehouse University and mentor to Martin Luther King Jr. Mays once said,

> Discrimination in the future will not be administered by poor whites and the people who believe in segregation, but by the "liberals" who believe in an integrated society. The Negro's battle for justice and equality in the future will be against the subtlety of our liberal friends who wine and dine in the swankiest hotels, work with us, and still discriminate against us when it comes to money and power. The battle must be won because, for a long time, the wealth of this nation will be in the hands of white Americans and not the Negroes. The problem of economic, political, and philanthropic discrimination is the first order of the day, not for the good of the Negro alone, but for the nation as a whole.[8]

Rutgers University professor Nancy Ditomoso makes a similar argument in her book *The American Non-Dilemma: Racial Inequality Without Racism*, in which she contends that racial inequality today is maintained through "opportunity hoarding." Ditomoso argues that, while most whites conceive of racism as people who harbor ill will toward nonwhites and who intentionally inflict harm on them, when we frame racism in this way it allows for whites to absolve themselves of the subtle and less obvious ways through which they are responsible for perpetuating racist harm. Indeed, racism today is more appropriately understood not as explicit anti-Black resentment but as whites having much greater and unequal access to opportunities, resources, and social capital. These are the things that ADOS specifically have always been (and continue to be) blocked from obtaining. Ditomoso writes,

"Whites can ignore the fact that most whites exchange favors with each other and provide the inside edge within the context of segregated communities, segregated churches, and segregated workplaces."[9] In other words, it is not what whites are doing *to* blacks that is the primary issue; it is what whites do *for each other* that ADOS are excluded from.

While Ditomoso is certainly right to point out the ways in which that unconscious exchange among whites consolidates advantage in their group to the exclusion of ADOS, that should not serve to minimize the power of the enduring myth of ADOS inferiority that informs many white people's opinions of our group. Indeed, whereas white people are often assumed qualified until they prove themselves not to be, with ADOS people it is exactly the opposite. We are assumed unqualified until we demonstrate ourselves otherwise.

There is an old axiom in the ADOS community that states how an ADOS person must always be twice as good as whites to get the job. And still, despite our best efforts to overcome that social deficit, we oftentimes find ourselves passed over for a position or an opportunity that is then given to a white person. We should never downplay or trivialize how those outcomes—which are a direct result of anti-ADOS bias—shape our self-perception and instill defeatist and self-hating attitudes *within* our group. Oppressed people must not only overcome their own self-doubt, but they must also overcome the doubt they feel for their fellow oppressed. And while it is frustrating and sad to hear how some ADOS hold such low and crude opinions of other ADOS people and our institutions, one is hardly shocked to learn they do. Anti-ADOS propaganda routinely reinforces those attitudes and does everything it can to conceal the true nature of why our people and our institutions struggle to provide the community with adequate resources. That is why liberation for ADOS must include a critical educational component on the ways in which the socioeconomic disadvantages we experience are manufactured things. They are not our people's fault! And ADOS must be conditioned to see all these deficiencies afflicting us as being purely the consequence of injustices that have placed us at a steep disadvantage. We must educate ourselves, and in so doing purge ourselves of doubt and uncertainty about our capacity to deliver the highest quality of goods and services. We cannot meaningfully press forward until we expel these persistent, white supremacist notions.

In the next chapter, we will see how this is precisely the issue that, in the post-Babylonian exilic period, Nehemiah faced upon his arrival in Jerusalem: That is, how do you get a people who have internalized self-defeat, and who have become so psychologically habituated to being at the bottom, to begin rebuilding? How do you empower the people? We will discuss the ways in which America has propagandized society into believing that that kind of work is no longer necessary for ADOS—that we have "arrived," so to speak, and already overcome the steep barriers that our ancestors faced in order to meaningfully participate in all areas of national life. Not unlike Nehemiah while he was in Babylon, many within our community have been lulled into a sense of complacency about our situation through false narratives that they have received about it. And yet, Nehemiah's political mission while he is in Jerusalem is, as we will see, one of such purpose! What, then, accounted for this marked shift in how he saw himself in relation to the plight of the Jerusalemites? Why the sudden awareness of the severity of his people's suffering along with a newfound sense of his responsibility to improve their conditions? What or who facilitated this radical consciousness, this infusion of Jewish-centric thought in which the interest of the Jerusalemites registered as his main priority? For ADOS today, these questions of how Nehemiah became reoriented in his thinking are critical to our own survival as a group.

Chapter Seven

Hanani's Mission to Expose Pseudo Innocence

Most of Us Ain't Movin' On Up

Nehemiah, I would argue, was precisely the type of individual earlier described in chapter 3. That is, he was a privileged Jew. And after being deported to Babylon, where he achieved a prominent position in society, he was content to be in service to the empire.

This is, admittedly, an unorthodox reading of Nehemiah. Religious scholars traditionally place him alongside Daniel, Zerubbabel, and Ezra, all of whom are rightfully regarded as Jewish patriots. Yet I believe this interpretation of Nehemiah elides the critical development of consciousness in his *becoming* the great and committed leader of his people that we, today, universally recognize him to be. Utilizing a hermeneutics of recuperation has been indispensable to my reading of the Scripture in general, and in my formulation of an ADOS theology in particular. As I pored over Scripture in search of the nuanced or less obvious issues taking place between the lines of text, it became apparent that perhaps no book of the Bible more so than Nehemiah's provides occasion for a rich discovery of such material. In it we encounter so many of the same dynamics of oppression that define the modern ADOS experience. And so, with an eye to that experience, I read the book of Nehemiah seeking to recover those aspects of the Scripture that would otherwise remain obscured but are important in their ability to speak powerfully to the oppressed group of which I am a part.

After all, if biblical orthodoxy in America reflects the interests and concerns of an elite and powerful group, then it seems preposterous to suppose that much effort has ever been applied to interpreting Scripture in a way that shines a light down a new pathway of emancipatory possibilities for ADOS. ADOS theology, then, proceeds from this recognition that religion has become an instrument in the maintenance of oppressive structures. It aims to tease out traces of the unseen that might help our group see ourselves most clearly; it aims to intervene and make the Word of God speak most meaningfully to our unique experience as a people.

Topmost among the relevant themes that surface throughout Nehemiah is something upon which we have already touched: the threat posed by integration when it is pursued at only the most superficial level. In other words, when integration is managed in such a way where only select representatives from the minority population are elevated, the group as a whole is left socially, politically, and economically dislocated and dependent on the dominant culture. With respect to prominent Jewish figures living in Babylon, we have—up until now—primarily focused on those who have resisted the temptation to disengage with the struggles of the remnant in Jerusalem. They achieved this through prayer and a constant affirmation of their Jewish heritage. This is not, however, Nehemiah's story.

As part of the second generation of Jews who had been deported to Babylon, Nehemiah was a privileged member from the oppressed group who served on King Artaxerxes's royal court. Nehemiah's role was that of chief cupbearer, one of the king's most trusted confidants. With the ever-present threat of the king being poisoned, the cupbearer was required to taste the king's drink before serving it to him. It is therefore difficult to imagine that Nehemiah, as a member from the oppressed group, would have been allowed to hold such an esteemed position had he not sufficiently demonstrated his allegiance to the oppressor of his people and assimilated in such a way that conveyed his complete identification with them. Indeed, when we first encounter Nehemiah, we do not find an advocate for the remnant of Jews in Jerusalem. Rather, we find a thoroughly de-radicalized Jew who has been experiencing the privileges of the empires that have historically oppressed his group. Nehemiah has received his political education first through the Babylonians and then later the Persians. As the royal cupbearer, his concerns are first and foremost those of the Persian Empire, and his enemies are anyone who is anti-Persian. The question for us, then, is how was Nehemiah brought to that epiphanic moment in which the advancement of his people became the paramount task? How does an elite Jew who has long enjoyed a privileged, executive position in the king's court experience such a sudden shock of conscience over the plight of his tribe?

The answer is his brother, Hanani. In Nehemiah 1, Hanani—accompanied by a delegation of Jews—has returned to Babylon from Jerusalem. When Nehemiah asks him about the conditions in Jerusalem, he responds, "The remnant who survived the exile are there in the province, in great trouble and disgrace. The wall of Jerusalem is broken down, and its gates are burned with fire" (Neh. 1:3 BSB). Sitting down to weep, Nehemiah is evidently greatly dismayed upon learning about the profound privation that the Jewish people are experiencing.

Of course, it is unlikely that this was the first time that Nehemiah had been given an account of Jerusalem. It is, however, quite likely that this report from Hanani constituted the first time that he was given an *honest* account of what was happening there. It is hard not to think that, heretofore, Nehemiah was told that the Jerusalemites were doing just fine. After all, at that time Jerusalem was dominated by Arabs and Samaritans, and so most of the reports that Nehemiah would have been receiving would be coming from Samaritan envoys whose local economies stood to benefit from Jerusalem's weakness. These envoys would have been bringing the "official" narrative, something that highlighted the power of the establishment story to mask the realities of one group's oppression.

Indeed, just as the Samaritan envoys concealed the true nature of Jewish life in Jerusalem—and just as Hitler during the 1936 Olympics in Munich hid from view the truths of Jewish oppression—America has long suppressed knowledge of the depths of ADOS suffering and pain. This has been achieved in large part through propaganda that presents our group to the rest of America as being largely unburdened by our history of enslavement and discrimination. In many ways, this sort of propaganda paints us as having no specific history at all! At the very least, our history in these renderings is certainly not one defined by a complete exclusion from the opportunity to ever participate as genuine equals in national life. In fact, it is almost as if following slavery we have always existed as equals in this country, a conceit that could obviously not be further from our group's truth.

But isn't the story of equality one that American society wants so very badly to believe? Of course, therein lies the very essence of propaganda: the creation of a certain (un)reality through images or messages that appeal to desires that are inconsistent with the actual data. Together, these things help to advance a false ideal of the reality the propaganda purports to represent to its audience. And indeed, the story about ADOS life that America wants to tell itself has become, over the years, increasingly *unreal*.

To gain a sense of America's desire to gloss and disguise the terrible reality that it has created for our group, we need only consider three popular television programs appearing between 1970 and 1990 that depicted ADOS life. The first is *Good Times*, which aired between 1974 and 1979. *Good Times* was the first two-parent ADOS sitcom to ever be broadcast in America, and it realistically dramatized the myriad struggles that an ADOS family would have been facing at the time. As a sitcom about ADOS life, *Good Times* was unusual in that it did reflect the contemporary economic reality of many of our people. As we will see, subsequent Black sitcoms appeared to elide that dimension of our group's experience.

In the show, the Evans family lives in Chicago's public housing in a poor neighborhood with very few amenities. When audiences tuned in to watch, they had an opportunity to really see the legacy of racism, generational poverty, redlining, and economic disinvestment that afflicted so many of America's urban areas. Moreover, they could see how an ADOS family struggled amid that confluence of immobilizing factors that have strangled the prospects of betterment for our group. Indeed, while there is an abundance of love and support within the Evans family, they nonetheless all must grapple with the fact of being made to live in a society that has so greatly limited access to opportunity for their group. In this regard, *Good Times* did not shy away from holding a mirror up to America.

But by the time we move on to *The Jeffersons*, which aired between 1975 and 1985, we can already see a significantly different picture of ADOS life that television studio executives wanted to present to audiences. The show portrays a middle-class Black husband and wife who have made their wealth as business owners servicing a poor, Black neighborhood. The core message of *The Jeffersons* is that previous discriminatory barriers to success have been removed for ADOS. And at the time, a viewer of the show might have easily surmised that access to historically white opportunities had indeed been opened to our group. The show's theme song, "Movin' On Up," is in fact an explicit reference to this notion of Black upward mobility.

Importantly, though, that capacity for ADOS to climb the social ladder a few rungs in the late 1970s and early 1980s was made possible by targeted government policy. And what audiences saw in *The Jeffersons* (whether they realized it or not) was the effect of affirmative action legislation like the 1968 Fair Housing Act that helped facilitate *some* ADOS moving from segregated neighborhoods into the suburban or urban spaces previously restricted to whites. These tenuous social gains for ADOS, however, would come under heavy attack during the Reagan administration of the 1980s. And ADOS, unlike no other group, would feel the brunt of regressive policies and small, conservative government ideology that sought to drastically cut the sort of social spending our community relied on in order to secure a foothold in a vehemently anti-ADOS society.

But while the harshness of our group's life grew more pronounced during that time—and the many ills of crushing, generational poverty started to proliferate in our communities—America kicked its propaganda machine into high gear with the airing of *The Cosby Show*, a sitcom that sought to mask those realities of ADOS life. Airing between 1984 and 1992, *The Cosby Show* portrayed the life of the Huxtables, a wildly successful ADOS family. Cliff, the patriarch, is a wealthy pediatrician, while his wife, Claire, is an attorney. In its depiction of contemporaneous ADOS life, the show would generate the impression among audiences that not only is white space now accessible to ADOS, our group has in fact become so successful that they occupy a socioeconomic stratum that even whites would have difficulty attaining. Social critic Antonio Moore notes that in 1984 the Huxtable's house would have been worth one million dollars. This fact is one that underscores the total *un*reality of *The Cosby Show*. As Moore points out, the Huxtables would have had to put down $175,000 on the house, and that house would—in today's money—be worth seven million dollars.[1]

Undergirding Moore's critique of *The Cosby Show* is the stark juxtaposition between the presentation of the Huxtables' life and what life was actually like for most ADOS during the time period. It was, after all, the time of Reaganomics, the crack cocaine epidemic, the beginnings of mass incarceration, and a trickle-down economics approach that in no way whatsoever benefitted ADOS communities. However, since the program so fits the description of emotionally targeted propaganda, *The Cosby Show* arguably never intended to depict that oppressive reality in the first place. Instead, the show's vision was a vision crafted for white America. It was a way to propagandize audiences both Black and white into believing that the United States had done away with its long-standing racial barriers to equal opportunity. No doubt that when white America tuned in to watch *The Cosby Show* in the mid-1980s, viewers must have wondered, "If the Huxtables can be so successful, then what is wrong with other Blacks?" If viewers saw that families in ADOS communities were—like the Evanses in *Good Times*—still trapped in poverty, then the Jeffersons and the Huxtables they were seeing on their television sets surely reassured them that it was not the system's fault. The Jeffersons and the Huxtables coddled white audiences with the belief that it was exclusively the fault of *those* poor families. And their pathetic situation reflected what white America has needed to believe all along: that ADOS life is what it is because of our group's apparent dysfunction and the absence of qualities like personal responsibility and a strong set of values. In this telling, the problem is no longer structural racism but instead the moral and cultural defects that are supposedly endemic to ADOS culture.

The Cosby Show, in other words, catered to a fantasy of racial progress and white innocence. And it is that latter psychological condition that has long been so essential to stalling the prospects of ADOS accessing the sort of opportunity that whites have always enjoyed in America. In 1967, when President Johnson commissioned a team of researchers chaired by Illinois governor Otto Kerner Jr. to identify the root causes of dissent that had been occurring in ADOS communities, the commission concluded unequivocally that "segregation and poverty have created in the racial ghetto a destructive environment *totally unknown to most white Americans*" (emphasis mine). The commission went on to say, "What white Americans have never fully understood—but what the Negro can never forget—is that white society is deeply implicated in the ghetto. White institutions created it, white institutions maintain it, and white society condones it."[2] The Kerner Commission's projected price tag for repairing the ADOS community would grow to be in the billions of dollars. And when we observe the massive success of *The Cosby Show* in the absence of any real repair in the lives of actual ADOS, we see just how eager white society has always been to forget. When the urban centers across America were rotting away due to white indifference, *The Cosby Show* offered a place where white audiences could safely retreat to reassure themselves of their innocence and ignore the fact that ADOS life was obviously so much different outside of a sitcom.

The propaganda we observe in our media landscape of so-called ADOS "progress" is but one example of society's preference for remaining ignorant of the extent and immediacy of ADOS oppression. In fact, all institutions in American society have long conspired to nourish what South African theologian Allan Boesak calls a "pseudo-innocence" in the people. The reason for that is simple: given the intentional pseudo-ignorance of the totality of exclusion that ADOS has been made to face throughout our time in America, it will be impossible for the nation to truly repent of the evils of racism, white supremacy, and grave economic injustice for which it is responsible. In the absence of that knowledge, white America will never be able to realize the extent to which their own advantage in this country is undeniably bound up in the history of our suffering and exclusion from it.

In his book *When Affirmative Action Was White*, Ira Katznelson reveals how the anti-ADOS implementation of Roosevelt's New Deal policies helped institutionalize preferences for whites in the postwar generation. Katznelson highlights the agreement that was reached between the northern Democrats and the southern segregationist wing of the Democratic Party, which effectively resulted in ADOS not being accorded the same benefits of citizenship in the United States as the white population. During the 1930s, the southern segregationists in Congress supported liberal spending policy because of the regional poverty that was then afflicting their states. However, that was contingent upon one thing: the matter of how those federal dollars were to be disbursed would be decided and managed by the states. And since these representatives were fully invested in the maintenance of the country's racial hierarchy, ADOS, of course, were thus systematically deprived of the relief that whites would (and did) benefit from.

For example, Social Security, it was decreed, was to be withheld from those individuals who held jobs in agricultural and domestic work, two sectors of the economy that contained nearly three-quarters of all ADOS workers in the South, and 85 percent of all ADOS women in the region.[3] Later in the postwar period, the US government would extend affordable home mortgages to whites in order to entice them to the suburbs. Naturally, the jobs, goods, and services then became suburbanized as well. For white America, this was a boost. But through restrictive covenants and de jure residential segregation, ADOS would be excluded from such prospects for suburban upward mobility. Instead, we would be contained to the ghettoes, where through the process of redlining—a ratings system created by banks that sought to evaluate the risk associated with providing loans in specific neighborhoods— we would be further deprived of economic investments in our own neighborhoods. Among the four categories of neighborhood quality that appraisers created, the red-colored portions on maps were meant to signal to investors that the areas ranked were the least desirable. They were, of course, ADOS neighborhoods. And even neighborhoods with relatively small percentages of ADOS residents were usually considered "hazardous." The upshot of this system was to motivate whites to maintain exclusively white neighborhoods in order to retain and grow their property values. And while white America was given yet another boost, there was— as always—the concomitant block for ADOS.

Because so much of this history of targeted exclusion has not been the topic of public discussion over the last several decades, many whites are under the impression that they have achieved success through individual effort, talent, and hard work. Most whites are entirely unaware of the legacy of white privilege and how it allows them greater access to resources and opportunities simply by virtue of their belonging to the group that controls those resources and that has such influence in providing the access to opportunities.

Indeed, when I think about the history of ADOS suffering in this country, and how white America has endeavored to conceal and suppress discussion of the extent to which our group's oppression and exploitation has made wealth and opportunity possible for other groups, it calls to mind the 1968 sci-fi film *Planet of the Apes*. No doubt *Planet of the Apes* addresses many of the prevailing themes of the geopolitically turbulent 1960s (during this era, anxieties over the consequences of nuclear proliferation and Cold War tension were particularly pitched). But ultimately, the movie is about why the covering up of history is so necessary in preserving the supposedly "natural" hierarchies of power in society.

Planet of the Apes transports viewers into a strange and unfamiliar world where the social order that we have known all our lives is turned completely upside down. There, apes are the dominant species and humans are the oppressed and enslaved. On this planet there is a section called the Forbidden Zone, a restricted area that neither apes nor humans may enter. All sectors of society on the planet—from civil to religious—caution against entering the area. And when the film's protagonist, George Taylor, eventually travels there, we finally understand why.

There in the Forbidden Zone, Taylor sees the Statue of Liberty partially protruding from the shore. And it is then that Taylor becomes aware of the planet's true history: that the unfamiliar planet is in fact Earth, which—after a nuclear explosion inverted the natural order—had come under domination by primates. And the reason for the Forbidden Zone being labeled as such a dangerous place is because of these very truths that it contains, the stories that it conceals, and the myths that it has the potential to explode.

Planet of the Apes provides audiences, above all, with an allegorical look at America's own motivations in covering up its racial history and shielding its population from the truth. Indeed, when it comes to that record of state-sponsored oppression and exploitation of ADOS, it is a pitiable fact that most Americans do not know what awful truths lay in our own Forbidden Zone. In some respects, most whites have been not only woefully ignorant in this respect but *willfully* ignorant. Much of white America simply does not want to know. More than mental ignorance, that unwillingness to be educated is a form of moral ignorance, and throughout our history we have always had morally ignorant purveyors of mistruths.

For instance, when Reconstruction ended—that first and in many ways sole attempt at healing the damage that the country had done to the ADOS population—a group called the Daughters of the Confederacy emerged. Determined to essentially rewrite America's racial history, the Daughters of the Confederacy undertook a nefarious campaign of ahistorical narration. It entailed three main objectives. The first was to convince the country that the Civil War had not been fought over slavery but rather that the war's catalyst was the matter of states' rights. The question, of course, that must be answered by states' rights proponents is this: What did the states want the right to do, exactly? Because insofar as they might claim that the right to own slaves was not the motivating factor in wishing to leave the Union, then they do so despite all evidence to the contrary. Indeed, in every Confederate state's statement of secession, the primacy of maintaining slavery was remarked upon. Alexander Hamilton Stevens, the vice president of the Confederacy, said in his Cornerstone Speech, "Our new government [rests] upon the great truth that the Negro is not equal to the white man; that slavery, submission to a superior race is his natural and normal condition. This, our new government, is the first, in the history of the world, based upon this great physical, philosophical and moral truth."[4] And so given this explicit defense of slavery being at the core of the Southern cause, it is indeed a wonder that the Daughters of the Confederacy would have the temerity to blatantly revise what lay at the root of the conflict.

The group's second objective, however, was just as false and even more obscene, for they ventured to persuade the population that slavery was in fact a benign institution, one in which ADOS had been treated humanely. Frederick Douglass, however, in a speech given on July 5, 1852, articulated what we all know to be the chilling contrast of that depiction of slavery. Acknowledging how the brutality of that institution was stitched into the very fabric of our republic, Douglass asked,

> What to the Slave is the Fourth of July? What! Am I to argue it is wrong to make men brutes, to rob them of their liberty, to work them without wages, to keep them ignorant of their relations to their fellow men, to beat them with sticks, to flay their flesh with the lash, to load their limbs with iron, to hunt them with dogs, to sell them at auction, to sunder their familiar, to knock out their teeth, to burn their flesh, to starve them into obedience and submission to their masters?[5]

Douglass's words here give lie to the narrative that the Daughters of the Confederacy sought to advance. Slavery's barbarism was unmistakable. It was not uncommon to read, in the description of escaped slaves that were published in local newspapers' reward notices, how that evil was literally branded onto the very bodies of those kept in bondage. "Twenty dollars reward," one such advertisement read, penned by South Carolinian slave owner Amber Ross. "Ran away from the subscriber, on the 14th instant, a negro girl named Molly. She is 16 or 17 years of age, slim made, lately branded on her left cheek, thus, "R," and a piece is taken off her left ear on the same side; the same letter is branded on the inside of both of her legs."[6]

To be excoriated then, to be set upon with a scalding iron and indelibly marked as proof of your ownership by another person— these are the features of the supposedly benign institution of slavery? These are the actions of a supposedly heroic and honorable people? Because therein lies the third objective of the Daughters of the Confederacy: to portray the Confederate soldiers as a band of morally just and supremely noble individuals. In this (re)imagining, they were to be understood as a people who had fought with great courage, against overwhelming odds, for a righteous cause. After the war, over seven hundred monuments would proliferate across the landscape of the South in order to preserve and uphold that narrative, a veritable crusade of propaganda again headed up by the Daughters of the Confederacy. They would then go on to lead a successful campaign to introduce all of this disinformation about America's history into the curriculums of schools throughout the country. In so doing, the young minds of this nation would be indoctrinated into an understanding of America's past that is wholly at odds with the reality (and the *centrality*) of our oppression to the making of the country. In mainstream culture, that truth is rarely the topic of movies or documentaries. And in its absence, most whites are quick to attribute Black underachievement to the "culture" of Blacks rather than the structural forces that have so grievously worked against our group's progress and achievement since the days that we were first brought to these shores.

An occasion comes to mind in which my colleague at Simmons College, Dr. Frank Smith, was soliciting a contribution to the college from a white donor. The donor wrote the check; however, he did not let the moment pass without offering a censure of the ADOS community. "My mother was a Dutch immigrant," he said, "and in one generation, we were able to assimilate into and succeed in America." Concluding, the donor rather callously stated to Dr. Smith, "You people need to get yourselves together."

What is revealed in this donor's remarks about the immigrant experience relative to the ADOS experience is an unawareness of how powerfully whiteness functions in America in terms of providing access to opportunity. When juxtaposed to a report that Herbert Hoover received during his presidency in the late 1920s (a full century before that donor would speak those words about immigrant assimilation and success), his remarks furthermore highlight how our society's ignorance on that topic has in fact gotten worse over time. The report states: "One notable difference appears between the immigrant and Negro population. In the case of the former, there is the possibility for escape, with improvement in the economic status in the second generation."[7] What the donor failed to realize was that because of the basic privileges conferred upon immigrants whose skin was not black, and who did not come from the history of exclusion that our group experiences, his family was able to assimilate into economic opportunity in America in a way that ADOS never could.

As has been stated previously, ADOS have simply never been given the opportunity of getting inside the "melting pot" of America. Our place has always been to serve as the firewood underneath that pot to get it boiling. We can no longer permit that just because there are some other Black folk now in the pot, the project of racial justice for ADOS is complete. No, for purposes of authentic justice, ADOS must be recognized by our unique designation. We must begin to focus on what ADOS life actually looks like when our group is parceled out from other "people of color," a catchall that necessarily captures a more economically diverse group of people and that is so detrimental to our particular justice claim. We need to go into America's

Forbidden Zone and exhume all that is buried there. Indeed, we can build up a sense of justice by breaking down that very word itself! For contained in it are all the awful forms that our oppression has taken during our time in America: J—Jim Crow, U—urban renewal, S—slavery, T—terrorism, I—incarceration, C—courts and cops, and E for that most enduring and harsh dimension of our group's experience—economic exclusion. This is the record of our suffering, and yet nowhere is our nation's unwillingness to meaningfully consider this record (and all that would be required to heal our group) more apparent than in the impasse with which H.R. 40 has been met.

H.R. 40 is a bill that Rep. John Conyers of Michigan first introduced in 1989. Having recently been reintroduced by Rep. Sheila Jackson Lee of Texas, the bill proposes to form a commission that would study the effects of slavery in America. And for over thirty years now, H.R. 40 has been unable to get out of committee. Moving the bill out of subcommittee would be the first step toward fulfilling a vision of meaningful justice that, as Walter Brueggemann has noted, is best represented by two ancient Hebrew words: *mishpat* and *tsedaqah*. *Mishpat* conceives of justice as entailing the equitable distribution of resources and goods so that all the members of the community might have a dignified life. *Tsedaqah*, on the other hand, is concerned with the active intervention on behalf of the victims of injustice and is meant to correct and repair those who have been specifically disadvantaged. To the extent that H.R. 40 aims at *tsedaqah*—to assess what is to be redistributed to ADOS and enact public policies and protections that help keep those resources in the community—then we cannot avoid striding forth into the Forbidden Zone. This would mean rejecting the myth of white exceptionalism as well as the myth that ADOS suffering is the result of inherent laziness and inferiority. It would mean confronting and overcoming the tension embodied in Allan Boesak's observation, "It is absolutely imperative for the oppressor to preserve their innocence, just as it is imperative for the oppressed to destroy it."[8]

White America will no doubt do all it can to avoid the Forbidden Zone. Because, as Boesak also argues, nourishing that (false) sense of blamelessness is essential in maintaining the status quo of white supremacy. Yet, in America, we will overlook a crucial point if we only understand whites to be the ones whose psychological disengagement from the struggles of ADOS perpetuates our oppression. Our group's ongoing oppression is undoubtedly also a consequence of our own leaders' detachment from our lived experience. And as we saw with Nehemiah in the beginning of this chapter, the status quo of one group's oppression functions most effectively when some of the members from that oppressed group are themselves so very complacent in their own privilege.

In the post-civil rights era, our leaders have too eagerly given themselves over to the comforts of Babylon while our group con- tinues to suffer in Jerusalem. And whether wittingly or unwit- tingly, our leaders, like Nehemiah, continue to go about their lives in a way that makes no real effort to connect with our strug- gle and help us overcome. We cannot wait around in idle hope that they suddenly come to the necessary revelation of our suf- fering for themselves. From our community must come forth the Hananis among us! Those truth tellers who are willing to express the present condition of our people and our grief unambiguously, fearlessly; we so desperately are in need of those whose insistent outcries against that injustice can then inspire and move those who are able to effect change.

Certainly, in pursuit of this justice we can anticipate much resistance. This was exactly what Nehemiah encountered when he sought the political restoration of Jerusalem. But our spirits must neither become deflated with worry nor too laden with the weight of setbacks that will also surely confront us in our journey. We must persist and exhibit great resolve in the face of all these things. "Follow justice and justice alone," Moses says in Deuteronomy 16:20 (NIV), "so that you may live and possess the land the LORD your God is giving to you." Because indeed, for those who dare to venture into this uncharted space of American history, there awaits a glorious thing: a revelation of who we are as a people, as a nation, and, of course, the promise of justice, of Christ. We must always continue to reveal the record of what we are owed. In so doing we will bring America to a place of great discovery and the possibility for renewal. And now, like then, when the record of our group's experience and all that we specifically are owed comes to light, we—like Nehemiah and the people of Judah—can begin that magnificent process of rebuilding and transformation.

Chapter Eight

Nehemiah Wept

ADOS Leaders Must Weep and Speak Up for Our Community

When I read the book of Nehemiah, I cannot help but be reminded of The Temptations' chart-topping single "Wish It Would Rain." In the song, we listen to a heartbroken man who, hoping to conceal his tears, desperately wishes that rain would start falling from the sky. I am certain that Nehemiah, who began to weep in Babylon upon learning the truth about his people in Jerusalem, also wished that it would rain.

As the king's cupbearer, Nehemiah worried that such evident and unexplained sorrow would arouse suspicion in the king. And indeed, when the king observed Nehemiah's distress and asked him what was troubling his spirit, we are told that Nehemiah was gripped with fear and said, "For I had never been sad in the king's presence."

In this response, Nehemiah betrayed a kind of consternation that today seems to afflict our own leadership in the ADOS community. Namely, that in being consumed with worry—or in letting the abysmal state of our group prey upon their spirits—they perhaps risk their elevated position. After all, do we not routinely observe an unwillingness by our leaders to extend the same degree of empathy for our people as they do for other marginalized and discriminated against groups? Not only that, it seems ADOS officials are expected to show great empathy for everyone *except* their own people. One example that comes to mind is when, during the Trump administration's policy of separating immigrant parents and their children at the US-Mexico border, many liberal and progressive politicians expressed outrage over the situation. Among them were many members of the Congressional Black Caucus. And while of course we ought to denounce such acts of obvious harm, we cannot help but notice how these same leaders have historically shown relatively little sympathy toward the millions of ADOS families who have been separated from one another because of mass incarceration. Haven't those policies— which encompass the pettiest of offenses, and which serve to exact the most incommensurate of sentences—worked to tear apart the ADOS families? What compels our ADOS officials to seal their lips about the myriad sufferings of our community? Is it some fear of reprimand? Is their reticence owed to an awareness that by speaking so specifically to the ravages stemming from anti-ADOSness, they might be setting themselves up for public criticism or censure? What are they so afraid of?

It is true that our elected officials find themselves in a similar predicament to Nehemiah, who faced the dilemma of how to be a patriotic Jew in the court of a king who was the oppressor of his people. Just as Nehemiah was very much afraid at the prospect of the king perceiving that empathy for his people had seized Nehemiah's conscience, so do our leaders appear anxious at expressing dismay and outrage at how the government has so mishandled meaningfully addressing the enduring legacy of chattel slavery. This is perhaps to be expected. There is a great probability of negative repercussions for speaking out against that aspect of our country. The point is not that these concerns aren't valid but rather that our representatives seem to lack the necessary courage to be willing to face those consequences and to say with complete conviction to those in power that our group faces unique systemic challenges and that we are deserving of unique advantages if we are to genuinely commit to eradicating institutionalized inequality.

Courage is all too often forsaken for careerism. What goes without saying is that our elected officials have not yet arrived at that intentional ethnic consciousness we see embodied by

Nehemiah. We instead find ourselves led by a pack of accidental and incidental ADOS. And in their seeking acceptance and approval from people outside our group, there can be no occasion that would force them to wrestle with the issue and find the resolve needed to fearlessly advocate for our group—to move towards intentionality. To be, in other words, sad *for us* in the king's presence.

In white spaces, it is acceptable (often it is encouraged) for ADOS to express rage over the oppression and marginalization of the LGBTQ community or of the mistreatment of people of color. It is acceptable for us to loudly declaim discrimination based on gender. However, when we raise our voices against the singularity of our own oppression—when we are seen as acting in no one's interest except our own—then we begin to trouble those waters of whiteness which, in America, must always be kept still and calm.

The most high-profile example of this in our culture in recent years was when former San Francisco quarterback Colin Kaepernick knelt during the national anthem to protest police killings of unarmed members of the Black community. Kaepernick did not allow the prospect of not receiving a paycheck to eclipse his troubled conscience, and he chose to identify before the nation first as a Black person—as someone who would not abide quietly while those in his community suffered—and secondly as a football player. The retaliatory action by the NFL was swift. Kaepernick's actions broke with what Devon Carbado and Mitu Gulati in their book *Acting White?: Rethinking Race in Post-Racial America* refer to as the concept of a "good black"—that is, a Black person who is always servile before an authority or a superior. In the league's banning Kaepernick from play, the NFL made it apparent that they would indeed prefer their Black players to think of themselves as purely "accidental" in their Blackness.

This is the game that white supremacy forces Black people to play. Never shall we too loudly express our pangs of spirit. We must always act in a way that placates the feelings of those who are content to watch our community be oppressed. For Kaepernick, in order to play one game, he had to go on playing this other. But what Nehemiah's experience of grief teaches us is that there are some woes so intense that despite a person's best efforts, they simply cannot be hidden; sometimes those woes inscribe themselves upon our very faces. Our leaders must not suppress and conceal their sadness at the state of our people; they must become conscious, ADOS-centric leaders who are committed to developing an ADOS political agenda that moves our group beyond equality to equity. Because while equality is everyone being treated the same, equity is everyone being treated *justly*. So often it is the case that white liberal reform efforts require ADOS to participate in noneconomic liberalism. However, any form of collaboration with any group wherein the goal is not ADOS economic empowerment and an improvement in our group's wealth positionality must be understood as wholly destructive to the ADOS agenda. We arrive at equity by way of an agenda that is driven primarily by the necessity of bringing wealth into the ADOS community. But the precondition to developing such an agenda is in defining who ADOS are as a group, who we are as a *specific* ethnicity in America. Only when we do this can we work toward moving ADOS past poverty, past our undercapitalization, past our being America's permanent underclass. Only then can we begin to rebuild.

In the next chapter, we will look at how Nehemiah cultivated this exact belief in the people of Israel. We will find him having spent nearly two months traveling to Jerusalem from the citadel of Susa—a journey again made possible only through government subsidies and protections (Neh. 2:8–9)—and discovering that the situation in Jerusalem proved even worse than what he had imagined. Indeed, so great was the ruined masonry and the heaps of debris and rubble, the donkey on which he rode was unable to pass into the city (Neh. 2:14). The gates of the wall that surrounded the city were all broken and charred by fire. And yet, the remarkable thing is that, as we will see, Nehemiah did not once become hopeless or surrender to the cowardice of pessimism. To put it another way, despite the devastation upon which he gazed, and which had existed for 150 years, Nehemiah did not become *rubble-focused*. Through his abiding faith in God, he staved off the cynicism that would otherwise have foreclosed on the possibility of repair. For indeed, whenever a person loses faith in God, he or she is sure to lose faith in others as well as in him- or herself. God was known to Nehemiah through this work of rebuilding his people. It was what God had "put into [his] heart to do" (Neh. 2:12). And that connection with God was so special precisely because it was not one borne out of the sort of miracle work seen throughout the book of Exodus (with the burning bushes, or the Red Sea parting, or the water coming forth from a rock). Indeed, in contrast to the book of Exodus, we find that the book of Nehemiah contains no such miracles! The sole miracle we will observe in Nehemiah is the miracle of believing in the possibilities of one's own people, of people "commit[ting] themselves to the common good" (Neh. 2:18). If Nehemiah provides an exemplary model of leadership through his organization of the people in repairing the wall around Jerusalem, then our first priority must be to do as he did: to first take up the work of repairing the *will* in the people. Let us now consider what our leaders will have to do in order to achieve this—to get the members of the community to a place where, as Nehemiah said of the Jerusalemites, "the people [have] a mind to work" (Neh. 4:6).

Chapter Nine

Nehemiah's Leadership

Mobilizing ADOS to Take Care of ADOS Business

What made Nehemiah such an inimitable leader was how he saw in the Jerusalemites precisely what the cynics and skeptics can never see in oppressed people. In fact, Nehemiah saw what the oppressed people *themselves* could not often see; that is, he saw the great potential that had lain dormant within them. He saw their ability to fulfill the promise of God's kingdom here on earth.

For it is God's kingdom that is antithetical to the philosophy of empire that has enslaved and oppressed people throughout history. When we speak the Lord's Prayer—when we say the words "for *yours* is the kingdom, the power, and the glory"—we must do so with full conviction in its bold defiance of empire's blasphemous claim to power and glory. Matthew 6:10 instructs us to pray "Your kingdom come. Your will be done, *on earth as it is in heaven*" (emphasis mine). That is a political prayer! That is revolutionary talk! And those words have always shaken and unsettled empire with their implication of establishing a countercultural movement in its midst and eradicating its rule.

It is not just the mere fact of a challenge to empire, however, that so disquiets it; it is *who* is doing the challenging. The kingdom of God always begins with those on the very bottom: the despised and the socially outcast. It begins, in other words, with the very people whom empire understands as being the most vulnerable to its power. But aren't the words in 1 Corinthians 1:26–31 a clear rebuke of this pretense of empire's power?

> Consider your own call, brothers and sisters; not many of you were wise by human standards, not many were power-ful, not many were of noble birth. But God chose what is foolish in the world to shame the wise; God chose what is weak in the world to shame the strong; God chose what is low and despised in the world, things that are not, to reduce to nothing things that are, so that no one might boast in the presence of God.

Nehemiah saw this design of God in the people of Jerusalem. He saw how they were to reveal the hubris of those who would oppress them and boast in the presence of God. Embodying the way in which God calls a great leader to summon the nobility and ability in ordinary people by loving them, trusting them, and believing in their God-given ability to do their best, Nehemiah preached to the people all the greatness that God had ordained for their group. In response, the call rose up from the enthusiastic crowd: "Let us start building!" (Neh. 2:18).

However, just as Zerubbabel and his workers before him faced resistance in their efforts to build, Nehemiah and the people whom he mobilized to begin rebuilding the wall around Jerusa-lem were also met with derision and ridicule led by Sanballat the Horonite, Tobiah the Ammonite, and Geshem the Arab, who represented the surrounding locales that controlled important trade routes along the Jordan River. Motivated by more than just a hatred of the Jews, Nehemiah's enemies were driven by the fact that any ascendancy by the Jerusalemites constituted a threat to their economic interests. The rebuilding of Jerusalem's walls sig-naled exactly that: a project of development that would undoubt-edly ripple outward and spur the local economy. It would allow the Jews to become empowered rivals in the region who could then pursue their own goals.

Israel's enemies' hatred and resistance was hardened by that felt anxiety of an emergent economic competitor in the region.

The imperative for them was to not allow the economically depressed community to develop themselves. They tried hurling insults at the workers to discourage them from building (Neh. 4:1–3). Under the leadership of Nehemiah, however, the will of the Jerusalemites was too strong, and they were undeterred. Nehemiah 3 provides us with a look at how Nehemiah—through his specific arrangement of the workers around the wall of the city—was able to strengthen the people's conviction in the work that they were doing. The priests, for example, were placed at the Sheep Gate, which was the gate closest to the temple. When sheep were brought into town for the sacrifice in the temple, it was that gate through which they would be led. This placement of a worker at a specific area of his or her interest is part of a pattern that is mentioned throughout the book of Nehemiah, and we repeatedly come across the phrases "opposite his house," or "each in front of their house" in the description of where the workers were making repairs to the wall. When we think about the future of ADOS repair work, our leaders would do well to look to Nehemiah and observe this relationship between the will of the people and their proximity to (and involvement in) the work itself. Nehemiah organized the work in this way because he recognized that such an important aspect of community development is how that development translates to the direct, economic empowerment of its residents. Therefore, by carefully having placed workers around the wall in a spot that was opposite their own homes, Nehemiah guaranteed that the activity that was taking place in a particular area directly benefitted them. He ensured that it was not just economic activity happening *around them.*

Nehemiah created such chemistry among the workers. He encouraged cooperation and contribution, all of which furthered the construction of the wall. The people had a mind to work not just because they were seeing improvement around their homes, but because they were being lifted up in the process as well. Among those who took part in the rebuilding of the wall were forty-one different groups, including priests, Levites, temple guards, goldsmiths, merchants, and private individuals. Women, too, were being enlisted in the work (Neh. 3:12). Although the wall was meant to protect the Jerusalemites, we read about how Jews from other areas outside Jerusalem—such as Jericho, Tekoa, Gideon, and Mizpah—came to help restore it. The array of workers engaged in the reconstruction of the wall, and the fact that the goal of completing a *common* task cut across the class lines that existed in Judean society at the time, attests to Nehemiah's ability as a motivator and his excellence as an administrator. Without that organizational skill, the attempts to motivate the people would have likely amounted to great frustration; the scorn that was heaped upon the Jerusalemites by their enemies might have proven disastrously more effective as opposed to it being a mere nuisance.

The workers eventually joined the sections of the wall, a feat that infuriated their enemies. Israel's enemies' disdain at the idea of an empowered Jerusalem then grew even greater, and they began to plot violence against the workers (Neh. 4:8). Upon learning about their intentions, Nehemiah urged his countrymen to defend themselves while bearing in mind that they would be fighting for their families: "After I looked these things over, I stood up and said to the nobles and the officials and the rest of the people, 'Do not be afraid of them. Remember the LORD, who is great and awesome, and fight for your kin, your sons, your daughters, your wives, and your homes'" (Neh. 4:14). As ADOS, we cannot fail to observe how Nehemiah is calling upon his people to fight *for* the things most important to them. He is not calling them simply to fight *against* the enemy. And when Nehemiah exhorted the people in this way, he meant to instill in them the notion that they would be fighting to create the kind of families and society that their children would want to be born into. Because these things—great families, great communities— do not just happen. Instead, as Martin Luther King Jr. once said, "Change does not roll in on the wheels of inevitability but comes through continuous struggle."[1] Therefore, if change is what we as ADOS desire, then what Nehemiah shows us is that we must directly involve ourselves in the heave and shove that will produce it!

This is, after all, how Christ reveals to us his goodness. Part of the grandeur of Christ's mind is to make goodness *positive* and not *negative*. By this I mean that in his design for us to become more Christlike, we have an active role to play. It necessitates us getting *into things* and not just staying *out of things*. Jesus always stressed that you cannot simply be "good" by adding up the things that you did not do, or by counting the bad things that you kept out of. And how could it ever be otherwise? After all, when you add up a column of one thousand zeroes, do you not still get zero? In the parable of the Good Samaritan, it is the Samaritan who is judged to be good because he *involves* himself in assisting the injured man. It is not the parable of the Good Priest, nor is it the parable of the Good Levite. Those two withheld themselves from helping the man. Similarly, in the parable of the Rich Man and Lazarus in Luke 16:19–31, Jesus tells us that the rich man went to hell because he didn't do anything for the poor man at his gate. And it is precisely such inaction that Jesus warns will account for how, in the time of the Last Judgment, some will find themselves accursed—not because they had done something bad, but because they had done nothing at all ("I was hungry and you did not feed me . . . ," Matt. 25:41–46).

Just as Nehemiah calls upon the people in Jerusalem to fight for something, so must we, in our fight to be more Christlike, be willing to sacrifice something of ourselves for the betterment of others. Nehemiah specifies that the fathers are to fight not only for those in their own generation but also for those in the next generation as well. One question that the older ADOS men and women must ask themselves in this moment is whether they are being good generational neighbors for their community's children and grandchildren. As a member of the boomer generation myself, I think the answer (it regrettably appears) is that we are not.

For too long we have not fought back against the sort of leadership that fails to prioritize our group's needs and our justice claim. Our failings in this regard have only intensified our condition in America's racial caste system. It is precisely because we have neglected to be good generational neighbors that ADOS is now engaged in a fight against an array of forces, from opportunist coalition seekers to corrupt ADOS leaders, all of whom do not want to see our people succeed and who support the kinds of policies that keep each new generation of ADOS poorer and poorer than the last.

This is exactly the kind of exploitative situation Nehemiah encountered upon his arrival in Jerusalem. For years prior, the rich nobles and rulers had been charging high interest to the poor Jews who—while working on rebuilding the wall—were unable to tend to their fields. The wealthy and powerful Jewish leaders then took the workers' children when those people could not afford to pay, and they sold them as slaves (Neh. 5:7–8). Combined with the external threat of Israel's enemies, this internal discord and dire economic situation threatened to completely collapse the project of repair that was being undertaken. To avoid this fate, and to deal with the wickedness and impiety of Jerusalem's nobles, Nehemiah convened a "great assembly" of leading men—chief priests, elders, and statesmen—who commanded that the stolen wealth from the poor be restored to them with interest (Neh. 5:11). The Jewish political and economic elite then signed a contract that bound them to this action of redistribution. Should they disobey it, the contract stipulated, they would be banned from Israel.

For his own governance over Jerusalem, Nehemiah completely eschewed the greedy practices that he said characterized the former officials who had abused their authority and who had brought the next generation of Jerusalemites into such a perilous condition. Nehemiah derived no wealth from the Jewish people's land, and he committed himself exclusively to the reconstruction of the wall that was meant to fortify his community. He declined to enrich himself through the office of governor that he held. And when, in the closing lines of the book of Nehemiah, he asks that God remember him for his acts of selflessness and "all that [he has] done for this people," we are able to see that what Nehemiah did for Jerusalem he had done out of no concern for himself. He had not set out to be revered by other people but rather to please God. And when it comes to traits that we need to be aware of when assessing leadership in the ADOS community, that sort of absence of ego embodied by Nehemiah is crucial.

We will continue, in the next chapter, to examine Nehemiah's leadership style by looking at it alongside one of the great unsung heroes of the American Black freedom struggle, Ella Jo Baker. Baker was the personification of the necessary lack of self-centeredness that we observe in Nehemiah. She in fact once said, "I have always thought what is needed is the development of people who are interested not in being leaders as much as in developing leadership in others."[2] In contrast to this style of leadership, which seeks to allocate power to the people and really cultivate and nurture a powerful emancipatory movement, we will bring into focus how a messianic style has largely defined Black movement politics since (and even during) the civil rights era, something that has proven so detrimental to our progress over the years.

Chapter Ten

Servants, Not Celebrities

Nehemiah, Ella Baker, and Exemplary Leadership for ADOS

Ella Baker embodied the fact that while Black men have been the face of the racial justice struggle, it is indeed women who have been the movement's backbone. Baker was a remarkable college-educated woman who was born in Norfolk, Virginia, in 1903. In the 1930s she became an employee of the NAACP, where she worked to establish and strengthen the organization's branches throughout the South. Having worked as a community organizer in the South, Baker had both the skills and the connections with the grassroots activists who were located throughout the region to help galvanize support for the NAACP. When tensions eventually flared between the NAACP and the Southern Christian Leadership Conference (owing to the NAACP leadership perceiving a threat to its membership and funding because of the stature of SCLC's president Martin Luther King Jr.), Bayard Rustin and Stanley Levison recommended Baker to help mitigate the friction. The SCLC, however, was an organization that was started by the Black church, and the Black church—particularly the Black Baptist church—was highly patriarchal and a rigidly sexist institution. Martin Luther King Jr. had expressed his misgivings about installing Baker as a coordinator because of the subordinate role that he believed women ought to play in relation to men. The organization, however, was in desperate need of her aptitude, and Baker was hired on an interim basis to run the SCLC from Atlanta.

Baker's leadership—however official or unofficial it was—proved invaluable. As coordinator of the SCLC's first official act (a kind of coming-out party), Baker played a pivotal role in organizing a joint Prayer Pilgrimage for Freedom with the NAACP. The prayer pilgrimage was held in Washington, DC, on May 17, 1957, a date that marked the third anniversary of the Supreme Court's *Brown v. Board* decision. Over twenty-five thousand people attended the SCLC-NAACP event, and afterward, President Eisenhower invited the leaders of the organization to meet with him. (It perhaps might not come as any great surprise that the person principally responsible for the joint prayer pilgrimage's success—Ella Baker—was not invited to attend.)

The following year, in 1958, Martin Luther King Jr. was stabbed by a deranged Black woman while he was autographing copies of his book *Stride Toward Freedom*. The attack was so severe that it nearly cost him his life. During his recuperation, Baker became the de facto leader of the SCLC. Despite her many gifts as an organizer and her dedication to the fight for racial justice, the rampant sexism within the SCLC precluded Baker from ever permanently taking over the role of the organization's executive director. Instead, a male pastor—John Tilley, from Baltimore—was hired to be the executive director. When Tilley was eventually terminated owing to his inability to balance the competing demands of his church and the SCLC, it was again Ella Baker who was brought in to pick up the slack as the organization's interim executive director. She continued in this role until the SCLC sought out a more "suitable" (which is to say, male) executive director, appointing Mr. Wyatt T. Walker as Baker's replacement.

The leadership structure of the SCLC would become a source of great consternation for Baker. More than just being sexist, its top-down nature effectively disempowered the very people who should have been benefitting the most: the struggling Black masses. Top-down leadership is when senior leadership makes the decisions and sets all of the goals and objectives. This style tends to be autocratic and creativity-stifling, and it inclines the group to passivity. Much like Nehemiah, Baker longed for a *group-based* leadership that was driven by the grassroots activists.

In the book of Nehemiah, we witness how Nehemiah had organized work so that the daughters of Shallum were functioning in a role that was traditionally reserved for men (Neh. 3:12). Nehemiah's was a nonsexist, egalitarian form of leadership that bucked the top-down approach in favor of a group-oriented effort at collective uplift. That top-down approach is nowhere more apparent in the book of Nehemiah than in the leading men of Tekoa, a group who stubbornly opposed taking part in the rebuilding of the wall around Jerusalem. These aristocrats from Tekoa "put not their necks to the work of their Lord" (Neh. 3:5 KJV). That phrase—"put not their necks to the work"—derives from an ox that refuses to submit to the yoking of his neck because the ox does not want to be controlled. For the nobility of the Tekoa, however, it was not simply the idea that the work that was taking place in Jerusalem was beneath them; rather, since they believed in a top-down leadership approach, they rejected the entire model that Nehemiah instituted in order to complete the work. The Tekoites believed in messianic or charismatic-centered leadership, a style that Norman Kelley in his book *The Head Negro in Charge: The Dead End of Black Politics* argues has long characterized ADOS politics.

Kelley cites the absence of organizational and institutional leadership in the Black community as the source of our group's intellectual and political class's ineffectiveness after 1960. With neither the organizational nor institutional leadership to undergird a movement and mobilize the masses independent of the Democratic Party, ADOS have thus become beholden to that entity's interests. Kelly writes,

> Black political culture tends to be charismatic, meaning that leadership is bestowed upon the individual possessing special gifts of the body or the spirit. In black America, the man (and it usually is a man) who can dynamically and expressively denote the mood or the will of African

Americans becomes a leader. . . . Charismatic leadership are men of the moment, usually a moment of great distress. When they leave, however, they do not leave behind patterns and practices that can be sustained over generations. Thus, today, black America tends to be organizationally weak as a result of its political culture being charismatically drenched by such leaders as King, Malcolm X, Jesse Jackson, Louis Farrakhan, and pseudo-charismatics like Al Sharpton. None of these men left behind or engendered strong organizations.[1]

In other words, for movements to be sustained, what is ultimately needed is not messianic individuals but messianic plans, strategies, agendas, organizations, and above all, *institutions*. The Black church, then, has an essential role to play in supporting the ADOS justice movement. Serving as the anchoring institution for the community, the church must do its part to advocate and agitate on behalf of the people. In his book *The Prophetic Imagination*, Walter Brueggemann states that the task of prophetic ministry is characterized by "criticizing and energizing."[2] That is, we must always criticize unjust conditions, and at the same time we must energize the people to dismantle them and construct a more just society in their place. What history shows us is that when the church leads the way in community development and justice work, then others are more inclined to get involved. And insofar as the Black church seeks to tend to the pressing concern of how we attract more millennials and Gen Zers, then the challenge with which we are necessarily confronted is how we become less like the leading men of Tekoa and more like Ella Baker, more like Nehemiah, and more like Jesus Christ. Because while Jesus is a messianic Lord, he was not a messianic leader.

In every organization you will encounter the leading men of Tekoa. The Head Negro in Charge is nothing new. They are the shirkers who criticize the workers. And from the first day that Nehemiah arrived in Jerusalem, the leading men of Tekoa sought to misinterpret everything Nehmiah did to advance his people. Themselves bitter, callous, and selfish, they imputed their littleness onto Nehemiah; they read their hearts into his motives. And instead of coming to propose, they came only to oppose.

It is critical to observe how Nehemiah wasted no energy on these detractors. Every leader only has so much energy to be applied to the cause, and it is essential not to waste it on trying to persuade those who do not want to be persuaded. Instead, a leader should aim to work with those who want to work and build power. The leading men of Tekoa may hurt your feelings, but they do not have to hurt your future. They are precisely the sort of people whose nonparticipation leads leaders astray from their main purpose. When leaders get so caught up with trying to involve the obstinate, the stubborn, and the pigheaded, they then neglect to focus on empowering those who are actually participating. I myself have been guilty of this. There was a time when attendance at the midweek service was quite low. Preposterously, I would complain to the ones who were in attendance about those who had not shown up! Wasn't it foolish of me to squander that time talking about those who were absent instead of empowering those who were present? Leaders must learn to move with the movers! We must, like Jesus, challenge them to do *more*. In John 14:12, Jesus tells his disciples that they would do greater things than he did. When Jesus said this, he was not saying that they would improve on the *quality* of what he did. Instead, they were being called on to improve the *quantity* of his work. This is what messianic leaders must enjoin and empower the people to do. So often when a leader is taken out by illness, death, or even scandal, the movement often is at risk to end with the passing of that leader, either physically or reputationally. When Moses died, many Hebrews believed that it was the end— not just of a chapter but of an entire book. The strong, charismatic leadership of Moses over forty years had weakened the will of the people; it had made them dependent and insecure. God reassured them by saying to Joshua, "Moses My servant is dead; so now arise, cross this Jordan" (Josh. 1:2 NASB). God had to assure Joshua, the successor to Moses, that while Moses was dead, God was not dead, the movement was not dead, and the dream was not dead.

In Joshua, more so than Moses, we gain a sense of a more democratic leader. We must recall that Moses loses his leadership position during a time when the people are desperate for water. God instructs Moses to speak to the rock and tells him that when he does as God has commanded, water will come gushing forth. However, instead of speaking to the rock as God tells him, Moses strikes the rock in a rage and says, "Listen, you rebels!" he shouted. "Must we bring you water from this rock?" (Num. 20:10 NLT). God sees Moses's response to the needs of the people as a breach in leadership protocols. In saying "Must *we* bring water out of this rock?" Moses is taking credit for doing what only God can do. Secondly, Moses is positioning himself as a messianic leader who must rescue and save the people.

By contrast, when Joshua is presented with a complaint by the tribes of Ephraim and Manasseh that the parcel of land they have been allocated is not commensurate with their greatness, he shows no such animosity toward the people. The truth is that Joshua has given them plenty of land, but the land is difficult to occupy because it is the land where giants are. He tells them, "You have many people and great strength. You shall not have just one allotment, because the hill country will be yours as well. It is a forest; clear it, and its farthest limits will be yours. Although the Canaanites have iron chariots, and although they are strong, you can drive them out" (see Josh. 17:14–18). What the tribes of Ephraim and Manasseh wanted were convenient blessings, but Joshua reminds them that a great people must be willing to assume great challenges. He refuses to give the two tribes an easier parcel of land, and he does not clear land for them. He empowers them to go up and take the wood country, which they successfully do. And in so doing, Joshua affirms the greatness of the two tribes.

Another way of looking at Joshua's approach to leadership (and this is something that we see very clearly in Nehemiah as well) is that he is committed to giving the people a sense of *somebodyness*. When Martin Luther King Jr. was once asked what he felt the greatest achievement of the civil rights movement was, he did not mention the groundbreaking legislation. Instead, King responded that the Negro had gotten a new sense of "somebodyness." King rightly noted how for centuries the Negro had been told that he was a nobody. And the real tragedy—more than being told that he was a nobody—was that *he believed it*. It was King's contention that the civil rights movement had caused the Negro to realize the vital necessity of rejecting that assumption, to raise one's back up, and to always recall that a man can't ride your back unless it is bent. A decade or so later, when James Cone would define Black Power as an "inward affirmation of the essential worth of blackness,"[3] we can easily discern the echo of King's articulation of how the civil rights movement had occasioned the recognition and assertion of the Black person in America's existence and the value of his or her individual self.

We know all too well the lengths to which white society will go in order to snuff out those feelings of self-affirmation. As Professor Carol Anderson says in her book *We Are Not Yet Equal*,

> The trigger for white rage, inevitably, is black advancement. It is not the mere presence of black people that is the problem; rather, it is blackness with ambition, with drive, with purpose, with aspirations, and with demands for full and equal citizenship. It is blackness that refuses to accept subjugation, to give up.[4]

The critical observation that Anderson makes is that white rage is triggered by black advancement; the dominant group is moved to hostility principally by the oppressed people's determination to succeed. This is also true of Nehemiah and his fellow wall builders. Their advancement threatened the prevailing social, economic, and political power structure of the region. And when Nehemiah's enemies' previous efforts failed to halt the progress that the workers were making on the wall, they attempted a last-ditch effort to lure him to a "reconciliation summit" on one of the plains of Ono. This is, of course, a farce. Their objective is to kidnap Nehemiah, neutralize the leadership, and eliminate the possibility for any further rehabilitation and empowerment of Jerusalem. Four times the demand comes for Nehemiah to go and meet with them. But four times he answers, "I am doing a great work and I cannot come down" (Neh. 6:3). This declaration is such a miracle in resolve, determination, and confidence. Nehemiah's great statement was saying three essential things about the work that he and the people were doing: the first was that the work of rebuilding the wall would be self-directed (I am doing); the second was that the work of rebuilding the wall would be self-defined (a great work); and the third is that the work of rebuilding the wall would be self-determined (I cannot come down). This unrelenting spirit to build must be what characterizes ADOS's political mission as we go forward. And when that determination so unsettles those in power that they try to lure us away from that mission and induce us with compromise, as Nehemiah's enemies had done to him (Neh. 6:2), let us always recall that powerful reply: "I am doing a great work. I cannot come down."

Neither can we as ADOS now come down. And what we require most of all are leaders like Nehemiah; we need people who are all so gripped by the high and noble purpose of doing radical, emancipatory Christianity that no obstacle can discourage them, no criticism can distract them, and no side issue can pull them down from doing our work of repair!

Conclusion

Beginning to Name Tenets of ADOS Theology

To understand how and why the Protestant Reformation of the sixteenth century sought to remake the foundations of faith is to understand why ADOS theology is so needed in this moment in America. In much the same way that the Reformation emerged in response to the excesses of Catholicism and the indulgences of the Catholic church, ADOS theology springs forth from a similar awareness that the institutions of our community are neglecting their historic purpose.

Over the last several decades, the Black church has undergone significant mission drift. What was once the primary institution in motivating and supporting our community to take political action in order to achieve genuine inclusion in America is now a shadow of its former self. And—to adapt a phrase from the great Frederick Douglass—as with institutions, so with people. In the same way that the Black church has decentered our group's singular struggle in favor of a more inclusive approach to uplift all marginalized populations, the people in our community have naturally responded in kind. For if our institutions are not anchored in our unique struggle, how then can the people whom those institutions serve possibly understand the primacy of our plight?

It is my hope that through this new application of Scripture the Black church can reorient itself and our congregations toward righteous action—that by moving away from an Exodus-centric style of evangelism and incorporating a postexilic model into our preaching, we as leaders in the Black church can impress upon our people the necessity of becoming self-interested in our political advocacy. To this end, I would encourage us to adopt a Reformation-like credo, a series of precepts that—when first introduced—were intended to distinguish its doctrine of salvation from that of the Roman Catholic Church. Those foundational tenets were *sola fide* (by faith alone), *sola scriptura* (by scripture alone), and *sola gratia* (by grace alone), and they governed Protestant theologians and clergy. For the Black church to once again become a force of great righteousness, it must break with our current Christian orthodoxy and proselytize the gospel in a way that grips its congregation with a clear recognition of all that we are facing in this moment.

For ADOS theology, the foundational tenets would be *sola* identification; that is, in an increasingly pluralistic society—with a growing number of Blacks whose families came to the United States from Africa after 1965 and the Caribbean—identification is paramount. How we differentiate ourselves from other Black people who do not share our particular experience of intergenerational exclusion is critical to the mission of bringing about justice for that condition. As we saw with Nehemiah, it was lineage that was the nonnegotiable factor in determining who would participate in the rebuilding of the temple in Jerusalem. When Nehemiah declared that God had "put into mine heart to gather together the nobles, and the rulers, and the people, that they might be reckoned by genealogy" (Neh. 7:5 KJV), we cannot but acknowledge the significance of lineage in God's design. It is the same with ADOS: *sola* lineage. And to the extent that we continue to take an interest in the affairs of others to the exclusion of those affairs most pertinent to our lineage, we then necessarily preserve a dimension of enslavement.

The Black church must not be ashamed to be the model for a *sola* Black institution: to concentrate on those things that specifically address ADOS. For it is so critically important that our community, and our children, be nurtured in a space where the concentration is on the singular experience of ADOS. I say this from personal experience. For me, the Black church was a refuge. When I was in middle school, I went to an all-white school. And there in that Babylonian-like environment I foundered. I did not achieve anything, and I internalized the attitudes about my supposed inability to succeed. The only thing that saved me was that there was a Black church to which I could go and gain an entirely different perspective of myself. The contrast that the Black church provided—this space in which Black people were everywhere, from the deacons, to the trustees, to the choir, and they were all celebrating and affirming me—changed the course of my life completely. So many of our Black youth today have never experienced that. They do not know that the Black church, as the mother of institutions in the Black community, serves a completely different function than the white church, that it is supposed to be the very wellspring of Black liberation and empowerment.

Beginning with the church, we must focus on strengthening all our institutions, for they are so essential to our survival. It is only when we have our own institutions that we can tell our own story. And how we tell our story is how we then shape policy and the direction for our community. In this respect, Black institutions must take the lead, for those who are closest to the problem are always the ones who are closest to the solution. When we think about the rebuilding of the wall in Jerusalem, we see how it was not accomplished by sending saviors into the community to do the work for the people. Rather, it was the Babylonian government giving resources to the right people *from the community* who knew how to use those resources to empower the people *in the community*. Like Nehemiah, we must begin with the assets that are already in the community and empower the people. That is what moves ADOS from being passive clients of white benevolence to becoming citizens who are self-determining and who are meaningfully participating in national life.

Lastly, and most importantly, there must be a *sola* reparations tenet in ADOS theology. Our situation, like that of the returned exiles, necessitates a refurnishing of all the wealth that was taken from us over the course of several generations. It is these three things—lineage, institutions, and reparations—that the Black church needs to foreground in its evangelism. In concert with one another, they are what will enable our group to identify all that we are, all that we are owed, and all that we can do. And so when we look at the road ahead, it is only right that the Black church take the first step in leading us toward that freedom, toward that promised land.

Acknowledgments

There are so many people whose support and encouragement made this book possible:

Yvette Carnell and Antonio Moore, founders and visionary leaders of the ADOS movement, provided me with the political education that helped me see Scripture through an ADOS lens. No one in the world is continuing the economic justice legacy of Dr. Martin Luther King Jr. in the twenty-first century like my dear colleagues Yvette and Antonio. I am so grateful for your groundbreaking work.

Much credit goes to Mr. Matt O'Brien: your advice and edits were critical to the crafting of this book. What white men like Thaddeus Stevens, Charles Summer, and John Brown were to the abolitionist movement of the nineteenth century, you, Matt, are to ADOS and reparations in the twenty-first century.

To David Maxwell of Westminster John Knox Press: your friendship, encouragement, and stern deadlines kept this writing project on point.

To St. Stephen Baptist Church, a solid rock of faith in action in our community: your embrace of a radical justice gospel welcomed and affirmed the preachings of a Jesus who makes reparations essential to racial reconciliation.

To Simmons College of Kentucky, America's comeback HBCU: many Black institutions have experienced mission shift;

however, you have remained steadfast in your commitment to advancing the ADOS movement.

A special thanks to my wife and life partner, Barnetta: your encouragement during my desert periods of writing motivated me to continue the journey.

Notes

Preface

1. Martin Luther King, "I've Been to the Mountaintop" (speech, Mason Temple, Memphis, TN, April 3, 1968).
2. According to Ira Berlin, 99 percent of all non-ADOS Blacks came to America after 1965, with 90 percent coming after 1980. This substantial segment of Black America—while no doubt victims of antiblackness in the United States—do not have the same justice claim as Blacks whose ancestors' exploited labor built so much of the nation's wealth. Ira Berlin, "The Changing Definition of African-American," *Smithsonian Magazine*, February 2010, https://www.smithsonianmag.com/history/the-changing -definition-of-african-american-4905887/.
3. Martin Luther King, *Where Do We Go from Here: Chaos or Community?* (Boston: Beacon Press, 2010), 39.
4. King, *Where Do We Go*, 54–55.
5. Jeanne Theoharis, "Don't Forget That Martin Luther King Jr. Was Once Denounced as an Extremist," *Time*, January 12, 2018, https://time .com/5099513/martin-luther-king-day-myths/.

Introduction

1. James H. Cone, *Black Theology and Black Power*, 50th anniversary ed. (Maryknoll, NY: Orbis Books, 2018), 37.
2. Antonio Moore, "Black Wealth in America Hardly Exists," Inequality .org, October 18, 2016, https://inequality.org/research/black-wealth -exists/.
3. Heather Long, "African Americans Are the Only U.S. Racial Group Earning Less than in 2000," *Los Angeles Times*, September 15, 2017,

https://www.latimes.com/business/la-fi-african-american-income
-20170915-story.html.

4. Cone, *Black Theology and Black Power*, 35.
5. Cone, 147.
6. Cone, 136.
7. Michael Eric Dyson, *Can You Hear Me Now?: The Inspiration, Wisdom, and Insight of Michael Eric Dyson* (New York: Basic Civitas Books, 2011), 187.
8. Dyson, 187.

Chapter 2: Solomon

1. Stokely Carmichael and Charles V. Hamilton, *Black Power: The Politics of Liberation in America* (New York: Vintage Books, 1992), 80.
2. Gary Rivlin, "The Blacks and the Browns," *Chicago Reader*, November 5, 1987, www.chicagoreader.com/chicago/the-blacks-and-the-browns /Content?oid=871364/.
3. Rivlin.
4. Dedrick Asante-Muhammed, "The Racial Wealth Divide in Chicago," Prosperity Now (formerly Corporation for Enterprise Development), January 2017, https://prosperitynow.org/files/PDFs/profiles/Racial _Wealth_Divide_in_Chicago_RWDI.pdf/.
5. Carmichael and Hamilton, *Black Power*, 80.

Chapter 5: Ezra

1. Monica Anderson, "A Rising Share of the U.S. Black Population Is Foreign Born," Pew Research Center, April 19, 2015, https://www .pewsocialtrends.org/2015/04/09/a-rising-share-of-the-u-s-black -population-is-foreign-born/.
2. "National Archives Displays the Refugee Act of 1980," National Archives (website), November 20, 2015, www.archives.gov/press/press -releases/2016/nr16-23.html.
3. "U.S. Diversity Visas Are Attracting Africa's Best and Brightest," Population Reference Bureau, July 1, 2001, www.prb.org/usdiversityvisasare attractingafricasbestandbrightest/.

Chapter 6: Esau

1. *Brown v. Board of Education*, 347 U.S. 483 (1954).
2. Dr. Curtis Woods et al., "Report on Slavery and Racism in the History of the Southern Baptist Theological Seminary," Southern Baptist Theological Seminary website, 2018, https://www.sbts.edu/southern-project/.
3. Writing for EthicsDaily.com, David Swartz juxtaposes the faculty of Southern Seminary's laudatory tribute to Brown, which described him as a man of "dignity and grace" who showed "courtesy to all," with the

decidedly less fond impression that the governor had left among many Black men in Georgia. Swartz writes, "Their recollections, which took the form of folk songs . . . went like this: 'Joe Brown, Joe Brown, / He's a mean white man, / He's a mean white man. / I know, honey, he put them shackles around, / Around my leg.'" See David Swartz, "Seminary Report Recounts Its Shameful Support of Slavery," Good Faith Media, January 23, 2019, https://goodfaithmedia.org/seminarys-report-recounts-its-shameful-support-of-slavery/.

4. "HBCU Facts," Cleveland Council of Black Colleges Alumni Association, accessed August 5, 2020, www.hbcualumnicle.com/hbcu-facts.html#:~:text=D.s%20are%20HBCUs/.

5. William Darity Jr., "The Case for Reparations," The Black American D.O.S. Caucus, 2019, www.blackamdoscaucus.com/kaliq-the-case-for-reparations-old/.

6. Augustus Hopkins Strong, *Systematic Theology*, vol. 3 (Philadelphia: Griffith and Rowland, 1909), https://www.gutenberg.org/files/45283/45283-h/45283-h.html/.

7. Altman K. Swihart, *Luther and the Lutheran Church, 1483–1960* (United Kingdom: Philosophical Library, 1960), 150.

8. Benjamin E. Mays, "Centennial Commencement Address," (speech, Morehouse College, Atlanta, GA, May 30, 1967).

9. Nancy DiTomaso, *The American Non-Dilemma: Racial Inequality without Racism* (New York: Russell Sage Foundation, 2013), 7.

Chapter 7: Hanani's Mission to Expose Pseudo Innocence

1. Eurweb, "Bill Cosby Sentenced to Prison: What Is the Legacy of the Cosby Show?," Apple News, September 25, 2018, https://eurweb.com/2018/09/25/bill-cosby-sentenced-to-prison-what-is-the-legacy-of-the-cosby-show-video/.

2. Otto Kerner, *The Kerner Report: The 1968 Report of the National Advisory Commission on Civil Disorders* (New York: Pantheon Books, 1988), 1, https://www.ncjrs.gov/pdffiles1/Digitization/8073NCJRS.pdf.

3. Meizhu Lui, et al., *The Color of Wealth: The Story behind the U.S. Racial Wealth Divide* (New York: New Press, 2006), 92.

4. Alexander Hamilton Stephens, "Cornerstone Speech" (speech, Savannah, GA, March 21, 1861), https://www.battlefields.org/learn/primary-sources/cornerstone-speech/.

5. Frederick Douglass, "What to the Slave Is the Fourth of July?" (speech, Rochester Ladies' Anti-Slavery Society, July 5, 1852).

6. Stephen S. Foster, *The Brotherhood of Thieves: Or, a True Picture of the American Church and Clergy* (Concord, NH: Parker Pillsbury, 1886; London, UK: Forgotten Books, 2015), 67. Citation refers to the Forgotten Books edition.

7. The Committee on Negro Housing, *Negro Housing: Report of the Committee on Negro Housing, Nannie H. Burroughs, Chairman* (Washington, DC: National Capital Press, 1932), https://archive.org/stream/negrohousing repo00presrich/negrohousingrepo00presrich_djvu.txt/.
8. Allan Boesak, *Farewell to Innocence: A Socio-Ethical Study on Black Theology and Black Power* (Eugene, OR: Wipf & Stock, 2015), 5.

Chapter 9: Nehemiah's Leadership

1. Martin Luther King, *Letter from Birmingham Jail/ I Have a Dream* (Logan, IA: Perfection Learning, 1990), 27.
2. Ella Baker, interview by Gerda Lerner, tape recording, December 1970, https://poweru.org/wp-content/uploads/2015/09/baker_leadership.pdf.

Chapter 10: Servants, Not Celebrities

1. Norman Kelley, *The Head Negro in Charge Syndrome: The Dead End of Black Politics* (New York: Nation Books/Avalon Publishing, 2004), 22.
2. Walter Brueggemann, *The Prophetic Imagination*, 40th anniversary ed. (Minneapolis: Augsburg Fortress, 2018), 9.
3. James H. Cone, *Black Theology and Black Power*, 50th anniversary ed. (Maryknoll, NY: Orbis Books, 2018), 4.
4. Tonya Bolden and Carol Anderson, *We Are Not Yet Equal: Understanding Our Racial Divide* (New York: Bloomsbury Publishing, 2020), 116.